POETRY DIVA

NEWLY FOUND
POEMS AND STORIES

Books by Linda J. Albertano and Frank Lutz

Poetry Diva

Two Souls Desperate to Connect with Help from a Third One

It All Began with Cherry Soup

On the Life of Linda J. Albertano: From Trauma to High Art

SKIN (Audiobook of Poetry)

The Linda J. Albertano Annual Fellowship

Founded in 1968, Beyond Baroque, the poetry heartbeat of Venice, California has established an annual fellowship that will continue Linda's commitment to supporting women poets and her spirit of artistic experimentation with music and performing arts.

Visit www.lindajalbertano.com to find out more.

- Writing scholarship
- A theatrical performance at Beyond Baroque
- Publication of your work
- Illustrious Alumni

POETRY DIVA

NEWLY FOUND POEMS AND STORIES

BY
LINDA J. ALBERTANO
AND
FRANK LUTZ

QUIET TIME PUBLISHING
Hollywood, California 90028

Poetry Diva: Newly Found Poems and Stories
Copyright © 2025 by Linda J. Albertano and Frank Lutz

All Rights Reserved
To reproduce or utilize this work, permission from the publisher, distributor or copyright owner is required, except for use in a review.

Authors: Linda J. Albertano and Frank Lutz
Title: Poetry Diva: Newly Found Poems and Stories

Library of Congress Control Number: 2025905475

ISBN: 978-1-884743-27-6 (Paperback)
ISBN: 978-1-884743-28-3 (E-book)

Subjects: Poetry, Fiction-Short Stories, Literature Collections, Music, Performing Arts, Film, Women's Rights, Politics, Narrative Poetry, Grieving, Afterlife

Cover images courtesy of Alexis Rhone Fancher

Book design: Kat Georges, KG Design International

Technical consultant: Alex Carmona

www.quiettimepublishing.com

The publisher does not assume responsibility for author or third-party websites or their content.

"I lovingly dedicate this book to my wife, Linda J. Albertano, a Los Angeles-designated Poetry Diva."

—*Frank Lutz*

TABLE OF CONTENTS

ACKNOWLEDGMENTS i
TOWER OF POWER: THE LIFE OF LINDA J. ALBERTANO iii
APOLOGIA ix
CRITICAL ACCLAIM FOR LINDA J. ALBERTANO x
REVIEWS xiii

Introduction xvii
Introduction to "Poetry Diva" xix
About the Authors of the Books xxiii
Linda's Women's Rights Bio xxiv

Poems 1
10-Point Plan For Female Emancipation. 2
Go, Carlye, Go! 5
Snakes on a Shark I 6
Snakes on a Shark Ii 7
Who Waits for You? 8
Birthday Poem for Regina 9

Politics, War And Peace 11
A 15-Point Plan for the Re-Establishment of Democracy in America 12
American Taliban. 16
An Open Letter to a Closed Administration 18
Busy (political) 20
Busy (performance). 21
Deluxe Damage (Roar) 24
Ice-Age Imperative. 25
Legalize. 26
LIONIZE 30
Martians Circle the Earth 31
Prepare for Peace 32
Responsible 36
Resurrection 37
Rhythm 39
Scenario #2. 39
Voting 42

Environment **43**
    The Courtship of Long Beach and Los Angeles Harbors 45
    Cranes 47
    How to Build a Catastrophe 48

Fun & Romance **49**
    Angelita Mia 51
    Para Francisco 53
    Para Francisco (Spanish) 54
    Dear Diary 55
    When Abelard Met Heloise 57
    Rattles and Gourds 59
    Senorita Bambina 60

History, so to speak **61**
    Being History 63
    The History of the N'goni 65
    World History 67
    Telephone Answering Device 68

Stories **69**
    Dolly / Dali / Dalai 71
    Favorite Memories of Beyond Baroque 74
    Fidelity 76
    La Vieja Loca 79
    AWOL from the Cancer War 82
    Pigtailed Noir 83
    The Shadow Knows 86
    That Ol' Black Magic 89
    The Last Malebasher 92
    The Cups 95
    My creative life 96

Songs **99**
    Brown's Trolley 101
    Dante's Inferno Blues 103
    Elena 105
    Jazz and Jurisprudence 106
    Jazz and Jurisprudence 107
    Jamie Hines 108

Miscellaneous **109**
    Burbling Martians 111
    Body Poem 112
    Experts 113
    For a Fallen Friend 114
    Message from Ted 116
    Shame 118
    Sleep 119

Invented Languages **121**
    Duck Chick Feney!! 123
    Remembering 2010 125

Works By Frank Lutz **127**
    Note from the author frank lutz about the following poem "This Place" 129
    This Place 130
    The Missing 131
    L'amour Pour Toujours 134
    . . . and you aren't there 137
    The Soft Spot 138
    The Walk 139
    What Was It Like? 140
    Who Was She? 141
    Yes, I Miss You Always 145
    The Love Ache 146
    We will . . . together 150
    No Sweet Voice to Call My Name 151
    One Last Amazing Story 152
    Easter Monday: Sicily, 1282 155

Linda J. Albertano Scholarship **169**
    Award Winner 171

Photos **173**

ACKNOWLEDGMENTS

I would like to thank the following people whose kind and loving support helped me deal with Linda's illness from the time we first knew about it in April 2022 to her passing in September 2022 and up to the present day, September 6, 2023. As of this date, it has been one year since our second wedding, held at UCLA Hospital, Santa Monica, CA, in Linda's room. The most joyous day of both of our lives. The saddest day came a week later, on September 13, 2022. Linda and I loved each other very much for well over fifty years. I apologize in advance if I omit anyone, I am grateful to you all.

In particular, I would like to thank certain people who loved Linda over man decades, and were devoted to her memory by helping me with various projects about and for her since she died, and continue to do so: Scott Wardlaw and family, and Alex Carmona, who have spent months sorting through Linda's bodies of work in four artistic disciplines—poetry, performance art, music, and film—in preparing those archives for delivery to the Getty Museum in Los Angeles. These folks also collaborated in making a beautiful film showing Linda in photographs and performance over more than fifty years of her life. Alex also has been instrumental in helping me with the book I have created about Linda's life in art.

Also, I would like to thank Charles and Tobi Duncan for helping me sort through Linda's personal effects and beautiful clothing, a very touching experience for all of us. I would also like to thank our ace bookkeeper, Bob Mitchell, who met Linda fifty years ago, and started a musical trio together, with Bob on the piano, and Linda on guitar and vocals. Also, I would like to thank Quentin Ring, Director of the world-famous poetry venue in Venice, Beyond Baroque, who has been instrumental in helping me craft the Linda J. Albertano Fellowship for Women Poets.

I would like to thank Deborah Granger, a good friend of ours for decades, who has been working diligently with me on editing the Linda book and brings several decades of her expertise in the book and creative arts milieu. Her creativity and discipline are invaluable to me and know no bounds! I want to express my sincere gratitude to Kat Georges and Peter Carlaftes for their creative book design, as well as Ashlyn Petro for the final review before publication.

In addition to the above, the following notable friends have been wonderful in their support of Linda's memory: Anna Homler, Nico & Hanne Mohl, Steve & Melissa Crothers, Joseph Staretski, Ole & Ulla Nielsen, Patricia McDonough, Sabrina Gilliard, Daniela Escamilla, Geri Cvitanovich, Rob Levy, Jean Caby, Des Walsh, Leslie Stanford, Bruce & Fran Peters, Greco Garcia, Nick Olaerts, Erin Blackwell, Bill Messmer, S.A. Griffin, Tom Fries, Taj Mahal, Ann Barton, Prince Diabate, Suzanne Lummis, Sheila Pinkel, Laurel Ann Bogen, Josie Roth, Elisha Shapiro, Cheryl & Bob Leathers, Gary & Cydney Man del, Keith & Ginette Koenig, Kennon Raines, Susan Hayden, Suzy Williams, Pegarty Long, Gerry Fialka, Keith Martin, Mauro Monteiro, David Rosenfeld.

I'd like to extend my thanks as well to the following artists for their essential contributions:
- Suzy Williams, singer extraordinaire
- Alexis Rhone Fancher, photographer
- Mark Savage, photographer
- Aline Smith, photographer
- Greg Tucker, Nearly Fatal Women photographer
- Pegarty Long's Philomenian, Venice Poetry Wall at Venice Beach photographer
- Keith Martin, photographer of Linda's last event at Los Angeles Public Library (Central Branch), August 13, 2022

On a final note, I express my gratitude to the friends who endorsed Linda's work and made a significant impact on her life. You will hear more about them in this book.

—*Frank Lutz*

TOWER OF POWER:
THE LIFE OF LINDA J. ALBERTANO

BY SUZANNE LUMMIS

SHE WAS LOS ANGELES'S veteran multi-disciplinary performance artist of the city's Second Wave (who'd found her calling when she studied with Rachel Rosenthal, a leading figure in Los Angeles's performance art movement's First Wave, in the '70s). She was a vocalist, musician and poet, or writer of poem-like things, speaker of witty, surrealist monologues and—together with her instructor, Kora master Prince Diabate—player of that difficult, many-stringed African instrument traditionally forbidden to women. People knew her famous height, 6' 4", but never her age. When asked, Linda Albertano always claimed she was 27 but had lived fast and hard [some say she was born in 1942; some say 1952]. The part about living was true. Wow, did she live, from Venice, California (her apartment complex stood just one block and one Pacific Coast Highway from the sand) to Vietnam, to Amsterdam, to Western Guinea. She performed in all these places, and more. She was Los Angeles's and she was the world's.

    Linda Albertano kept packing in experience and delivering experiences to others until age *(cough, cough)*, September 13, 2022. Frank Lutz, her partner of fifty-five years—then, in the last days of her life, husband—has this fall endowed Beyond Baroque Literary Arts Center in Venice a fellowship in her name, an endowment to enable women to study, tuition free, poetry writing with an accent on the art of performance, *The Linda J. Albertano Fellowship for Women Poets*.

Note: This article originally appeared in the April 2025 issue of *Poetry Flash*

POETRY DIVA

What is the most interesting set of facts about the late, but recent, multi-disciplinary performance artist Linda J. Albertano? Is it . . .

A:
That in the late 1960s, she arrived in L.A. on a Greyhound Bus with $50 in her pocket, knowing no one, but with her impressive height and a presence to go with it landed a job at Disneyland as Space Girl, host to Tomorrowland, and then as a silent Greek goddess representing Colgate-Palmolive, taught herself the guitar, played coffee houses, got a student loan to go to UCLA film school and supplemented it by waitressing, working as a map librarian and teaching guitar, toured Vietnam and South Korea with other entertainers for USO, then in the late '70s, went through a life changing, life discovering experience when she studied experimental performance techniques with Rachel Rosenthal, a seminal figure in Los Angeles's Women's Art Movement. After that coming-of-age, Linda landed the role of *Evil Nurse and Executioner* and toured with the most transgressive, and successful, rockstar of the day. Among other transgressions, in each show Linda Albertano, in full frightening face paint, enacted piercing the neck of screaming Alice Cooper with a syringe of liquid. All in good fun, of course.

Now, a confident performer and creator of her own shows, with a style like no one else's, humorous, serious, wonderfully and wildly inventive yet highly disciplined, in 1994, together with Wanda Coleman, Lydia Lunch and Exene Cervenka, she represented the innovative end of the L.A. art scene at the One World Poetry Festival in Amsterdam.

She got great reviews, including one in this publication:
> "Linda Albertano, a very tall, striking blonde with fine eyes, was softer, more modulated, with a genuine, avant-garde café style. She gave a riveting performance of monologues in a tough vernacular."
> —Harold Norse, *Poetry Flash*, January 1985

Or, *is it . . .*

B:
1) That over the years, for holidays, birthdays, or no particular occasion, I went to dozens of movies with Linda, often with Laurel Ann Bogen, the other member of our seriocomic performance trio, Nearly Fatal Women, and she loved all of

them. Or, more accurately, she found something to enjoy in all of them. And what a variety of movies we attended, the first in New York City, Paul Thomas Anderson's *Boogie Nights*, exploring characters rising or falling to ruin in a lucrative but unsavory business, and more recently the sweetly optimistic full-length movie of *The Crown* saga, in which the royal family enters the jazz age, and for one holiday, a black and white movie from 1965—one of the last of the poverty-budget black and white movies before the rise of "arty" black and white movies— The Train, with Burt Lancaster as a railroad operator charged with stopping the Nazis from stealing the great art of Paris—that one on DVD. During the pandemic when we couldn't get together we streamed or DVD'ed a double bill in our separate homes, a comic version of the Faustian tale where a hopelessly in love fry cook (Dudley Moore) sells his soul to the devil (Peter Cook), *Bedazzled* (1969), and in the same afternoon, *The Sapphires* (1913), based on a true story of four indigenous women of Australia who in the 1960s, against much social resistance, skepticism, and with few prior models and no Phil Specter, resolve to form a Motown singing group. After we watched those, we discussed both movies with great relish—on Zoom.

    She liked those widely contrasting shows, and many others, or found something to like in each. And, in each case, she could say exactly what she liked, and why.

2) Over the years, we must have gone out for 100 meals, *at least*, pasta dishes and bowls of noodles, Mediterranean, Tex-Mex, and all-American, coffee house food and bistro and budget-fancy, and down in San Clemente, crab stuffed sole, sea bass with plum sauce, tagine of antelope. And a few doors down from the Village Mediterranean (now closed for good—I just found out), cashew butter chews and violet butterfly shaped confections at Schmitt's Belgian Chocolate. I don't recall that she ever had a meal she didn't enjoy, though she once regretted that she'd chosen chicken mole instead of something more adventurous.

3) When I think of Linda, before I remember things she said, before I remember her performances or our performance collaborations, before I remember her rare musicianship on the Kora with Prince Diabate, I hear her laughter. She found humor in many things, but it wasn't just wit or punch lines or the absurd that made her laugh. It was the joy of life. There are many types of laughter, hers

was the laughter of delight. Everyone who knew Linda Albertano and who reads this knows just what I mean. Already they are nodding.

Both blocks of bio information are interesting, but both become even more so with . . .

C:
Before Linda had turned seven, she was taken from her alcoholic and not-altogether-competent mother and deposited into the foster care system where her situation became far worse, fast—she was used as an unpaid, unloved household servant in foster homes, families of fundamentalist and Evangelical Christians. "Christians." (Is it time yet to drop the *Christ* and just call such people, I mean the type of people I'm about to describe, *ians*?) In most of these homes she was forbidden to join in the family's conversations. She was forbidden even to speak. In one household, Linda told me, she was referred to as "it," and "that thing," as in "go tell that thing to bring me some coffee." In one, the matriarch confined her to her room for some days and told her, "I'd kill you, but I don't want to face the consequences."

She was a child, and not a particularly rebellious one—she remained silent and cowed. Then she was a teenager, still with no home of her own, still among people who drilled her with Bible studies but despised her because she was not one of *them*. However, they liked the increments of money they got for keeping her and the free labor.

It was around the time she returned from the Vietnam tour and began again working as a waitress that Linda says the oppression and loneliness of her childhood surfaced and got a grip on her. In a recent piece in *VoyageLA Magazine* she addresses this: "At that point, the knot of fear and rage inside me began to erupt into suicidal tendencies. I was fortunate enough to find a caring therapist at Suicide Prevention Clinic who counseled me three times a week for over two years at no cost."

A turning point came when she enrolled at UCLA. "Once again, I was lucky! Because I'd been forbidden to speak in my formative years, creativity became my outlet, my permission to speak. And I really didn't care what form it took . . . Performance Artist, Musician, Spoken Word Artist. I was so happy to be released from the gulag that these expressions simply poured out of me."

Even then, more stripping away of early trauma was required, although at each obstacle, through strength of character and a little luck, she turned her vulnerabilities to her advantage. She discovered she couldn't convince performance venues to give her a solo shot, "Even with a portfolio of glowing reviews from *The L.A. Times*, *Art Week*, and P*oetry Flash* I was brutally dismissed. I finally realized that because I was trained to be ashamed to ask for anything, they only saw the cringing, fearful thirteen-year-old inside me. So, I performed in other artists' pieces and waited to be invited to do my own solos. Which worked well because I was eventually sought out."

Most specifically, writers of the Los Angeles poetry monde sought her out—Linda told me this not long after we got to know each other. She hadn't billed herself as a poet, yet it was poets who embraced her. However, we didn't get to know each other the first time I saw, heard her, sometime after her Alice Cooper tour and the One World Festival in Amsterdam. I was in the lobby of a theater in East Hollywood, and on stage, among other poets who'd read from their manuscripts-in-progress, a statuesque blonde woman was now up there doing interesting things with language, mini-performances with humor and bite that negotiated between theater and dream, punctuated with totemic movements. However, at that age, that long ago, I was probably feeling snobbish—*at first*. Knowing me, knowing me as I was *then*.—Because I'd studied with Philip Levine and Mark Strand, and she hadn't.

I got over that. Remarkable what one can overcome.

Readers will understand now why I promised "C" would deepen and enhance the significance of "A" and "B." After years of enforced silence and isolation (in some households she was not even allowed to have friends), when finally released into the wide, various world, and finally delivered from her own psychic damage, she seized the bounty of life. She seized it every which way and from all directions.

I'm not sure that Linda Albertano feared anything at all except religious zealots. She feared Mike Pence more than Donald Trump. We argued a bit about that—I told her 'Don't you see, Trump's followers don't give a damn about Pence or his religion, they're fanatics for just one brutal, stupid man.' Small wonder she had a horror of the soft-seeming Mike Pence and his trimmed salt-white hair, and his literalist reading of the Bible. But oh and OMG, what chills she'd get from the new House Speaker . . . Demonic, shrieking Alice Cooper in blood-splattered straitjacket, eyes rimmed in black grease paint didn't unsettle her, but Puritan style religious enforcer Mike Johnson with his Clark Kent eyeglasses and the look of a CPA would give her nightmares.

When Linda was in the hospital, and it was the end-game—cancer—she and Frank Lutz looked at each other and . . . Neither remembered who said it first—let's get married. Through a smartphone search they reached an accommodating person, a Russian Jewish person from New York City, who reminded Frank pleasantly of other Russian Jewish people of New York City. He was qualified to officiate and was available on short notice, as in *now*. Then they called in a friend to witness, and had the ceremony, the short version. After their vows, Frank said, they began to laugh, then they sobbed together, then laughed again, laughed like kids. Linda would have three more days to live. Frank told me, "It was the happiest day of our lives."

In a 1984 *Los Angeles Times* profile, Linda J. Albertano told Richard Cromelin, "I don't know why I should be an evangelist for people to get more out of our journey through this little vale. I just feel people aren't getting the juice out of life . . ."

How like Linda to keep getting the juice out of life, straight up to the end.

Suzanne Lummis is a poet, teacher, arts organizer, and impresario in Los Angeles. Her most recent collection is Open Twenty-Four Hours. *She is associated with poem noir, and the literary incarnation of performance poetry—the Stand-up Poetry of the '80s and '90s.*

APOLOGIA

Dear Reader,

To all the talented photographers who captured breathtaking images of Linda for this book about her life, we, the author, editors, publisher, and technicians involved in its creation, sincerely apologize for not having a record of your names.

Prior to her departure, Linda left a pile of photos, newspaper articles, and reviews of her performances and readings on her desk. Unbeknownst to Frank, she indirectly communicated to him her intention to pursue their shared dream of creating a poetry book. Although she is not here, we present this book on her life with a mix of sorrow and happiness.

Linda performs "To the Pacific" at the Venice Poet's Wall Monument, just steps from the sand along the boardwalk.

City of Los Angeles

Certificate of Recognition
is hereby presented to

Linda J. Albertano

POETRY DIVA

HONORING HER PARTICIPATION IN THE VENICE PEOPLE'S CENTENNIAL "DIVAS OF VENICE" SHOWCASE, WHICH REFLECTS AND CELEBRATES THE DIVERSITY AND UNIQUENESS OF EXTRAORDINARY VENICE WOMEN.

AUGUST 5, 2005

PRESENTED BY

Bill Rosendahl
BILL ROSENDAHL
Councilmember 11th District

CRITICAL ACCLAIM FOR LINDA J. ALBERTANO

SUZANNE LUMMIS
(Founding Member of Nearly Fatal Women, poet, professor, and author)
After we've noted that Linda J. Albertano thrived in Los Angeles as a force of nature and fount of mischievous intelligence and performative creations; after we've remarked upon the ways she seemed always larger than life, as well as—at 6'4"—taller than most; after we've marveled at her triumphant career in the edgiest art despite being silenced, abused, and exploited in Evangelical and Fundamentalist Christian foster homes during much of her youth . . .

LAUREL ANN BOGEN
(Founding Member of Nearly Fatal Women, poet, professor, and author)
Linda Albertano, a force of nature, a woman of integrity, a singular voice of unimpeachable honesty. A goddess who rose from childhood trauma and created art that left audiences breathless. She was my friend. Always.

S.A. GRIFFIN, POET, ACTOR, AND DADAIST SUPREME
A deeply compassionate and transformative performance artist and poet-writer, Linda J. Albertano was without peer. It is impossible not to be touched by the magic of her boundless humanity and love for all.

ANNA HOMLER, POET AND PERFORMANCE ARTIST
She was an awe-inspiring presence, performance poet and film maker. Linda was a great soul, larger than life and utterly brilliant. She was infinitely kind and utterly brilliant. Life will never be the same without her. Dearest Linda, in your own words, "I will worship at your shrine, forever."

QUENTIN RING, DIRECTOR, BEYOND BAROQUE
Whether you knew Linda from her utterly original performance art, or from her kora playing, or from hearing her read, or from simply spending time with her in conversation, she was always truly a poet. She breathed life into language, and expanded our sense of what is possible. She has left her poems as a gift to us all, and for that I am truly thankful. They will continue to transform the imaginations of all of us who encounter them.

TAJ MAHAL
Great Blues Artist

If there ever was a Creative, Very Feminine, Amazon Goddess of the sweetest nature & temperament that this or any other world has ever seen or known, it has to have been my dear musical friend, the late Linda "Albert" Albertano.
Always smiling and happy, so much so
even her laughter sparkled with musical notes!
Moving with the ancient grace of a gazelle, I never once saw her
compromise her glorious height with no man, woman,
child or musician!
Absolutely stunning
woman!
She wrote volumes of poetry, songs, was a wonderful performance artist,
played guitar, sang
and so much more!
I was recently able to play one of my all time favorite songs of Linda's, called "2:10 Train"
This concert, which featured The Taj Mahal Quartet and a
very lovely friend from both our pasts named Pamela Poland!
The combination of the quartet, Pamela's strong performance, warm and soothing voice & vocal, mesmerized
the sold out audience!
They responded with thunderous applause!
Thrilled doesn't even come close to how it felt!
We KNOW SHE heard us!!:))
Peace & Beauty
(Rest In Power)

PRINCE DIABATE, KORA MASTER GUINEA, WEST AFRICA
(Translated from the French by Frank Lutz.)
For my Big Sister Linda J. Albertano, my advisor, my student, she was a Grand Lady, very special in my life. I am composing your song, my sister Linda's song in the Zone of the Spirit and with us. Thank you very much, my Linda, from my heart, and with gratitude. Your kora instructor since 1999.

Prince Diabate, is known in Africa as Kora Master

ADAM LEIPZIG
Producer, director, stage, and performance art productions
When we opened the Los Angeles Theatre Center in 1985, performance art had already matured and was moving forward along different and divergent pathways. We had to do a performance art series and we had to get Linda J. Albertano. Linda was flattered to be asked, surprised even, which surprised me, because I had only seen her in performance, and her work struck me as so singular she'd be difficult to convince. "What do you do there?" Linda asked me. "I'm the dramaturg and producing this series," I said. "Of course I'll do it," said Linda. She even knew what a dramaturg was!

Of performance art's divergent pathways at the time, Linda had made the unequivocal decision for performance. She talked, she sang, she moved. She spoke poetry, changed costumes and characters. She had the capacity concentrate herself and expand herself into each situation. When she concentrated herself, her body reduced, became smaller and more vulnerable. This was part of her art, because in life she was taller than most everyone around. When she expanded, you could have sworn she was eight feet tall.

Did I mention the marching band? Yes, there was a marching band. Thirty high schoolers from South LA, dancers, and poets too, all brought together by Linda for her epic piece "Joan of Compton." The band was out in front on Spring Street, drums beating time as they warmed up. Across the street, windows opened at the Alexandria Hotel, a hotel that had once been grand but was now SRO, windows opened, curses hurled, empty 7 Crown bottles hurled too, glass shattered everywhere. We brought the band inside, and Joan of Compton went on. This performance of identity and sacrifice, interrogating the role of women, of suburbs' contrast with central city, of self-realization and self-abnegation being a white person in diverse society.

Where was the truest performance, Linda wondered later, in our 99-seat black box theatre, or in the glass on asphalt outside?

In more recent years we had the privilege of publishing some of Linda's poems in Cultural Daily, and her memories of performing for USO in Vietnam. Whether in words written or spoken, in poetry or prose, in music and in physical presence, her light transcended shape and form. That was her pathway!

PETER CARLAFTES & KAT GEORGES
Poets, publishers and leaders in the Dada art movement

Linda Albertano was a one-of-a-kind artist and human being. Her poetry and performance art was so earth-shatteringly original, it made us all aspire to raise the stakes of our own work. But an artist is more than their art, and Linda was equally defined by her kindness, her humor, and her indefatigable support of other creators. For many years, Linda has been a beloved member of our worldwide Dada family, performing with us in Los Angeles, San Francisco, and New Orleans, with original work, in a staged reading, embodying New York Dada legend Baroness Elsa von Freytag Loringhoven, and more. We miss her daily, and thrive on the memory of our time together.

REVIEWS

"Linda J. Albertano was "a musician, a storyteller, a displayer of props, a comically-generated presence, a model of complex speaking methods, and a performance artist whose work has been presented in Europe as well as America."
—**Benjamin Weissman, Beyond Baroque**

"The magnetic personality and majestic presence of Linda Albertano is depicted through photos and poetry in this wonderful biography."
—**Mary Goodfader, Small World Books, Venice, CA**

"A genuine avant-garde café style . . . a riveting performance of monologues."
—**Harold Norse,** *Poetry Flash*

"With satire and simile as her tools, she unravels scenarios, attempting to uncover their subtexts . . . A commentary that entertains and educates as it inquires."
—**Julie Taraska,** *LA Weekly*

"Linda Albertano creates a peculiar personal montage of love and politics on both sides of the board . . . "
—**KCRW Santa Monica**

"Linda Albertano in her own right managed to carve out a niche of her own . . . "
—*Los Angeles Times*

"Her work resembles songs, tiny pieces of modern love that cut like a knife . . . "
—*L.A. Weekly*

"On stage, Linda Albertano rivets with her astute observations of life on the edge."
—*The Best of L.A.'s City Life*

"This time around, her smart-talking cabaret style performance was out there for all the see under the sky and sun, on the Santa Monica beach . . . "
—**Santa Monica Bay News**

"Sexual and political power relations form Albertano's stomping ground . . . "

—*The Wire (UK)*

MEET POETRY DIVA
LINDA J. ALBERTANO

PERFORMANCE BIO

Linda J. Albertano was a phenomenon from the 1960s to the 2020s. She graduated from UCLA film school before studying performance with cultural icon Rachel Rosenthal and plunging headlong into inter-media performance. This she unleashed in such major venues as **The LA Theater Center**, UCLA's **Schoenberg Hall**, **The John Anson Ford Theater**, **Barnsdall Gallery**, as well as San Francisco's **New Langton Arts** and San Diego's **Sushi Gallery** (among others). During the same period, she often found herself reading her bare text in the company of poets. She's been featured frequently at **Beyond Baroque**, **SPARC**, **LACE**, **Highways**, and other literary/spoken word meccas. She's read her work at literally hundreds of events, appearing in such diverse contexts as Sunday Services at **The Church in Ocean Park**, MTV's **The Cutting Edge**, **LA's Blue-Line** rapid-transit, various colleges and universities (including the Universities of California at Los Angeles, Long Beach, and Irvine) and an assortment of serious venues like **Galeria Ocaso** and **The Lhasa Club**, or rowdy rock'n'roll palaces like **The Knitting Factory** (LA and NY) and **Club Lingerie**. She's delivered her text at the **LA Poetry Festival**, **South by Southwest**, **Lollapalooza**, **WORD LA**, and **ALLEN GINSBERG'S AMERICA** (his memorial celebration), as well as places in Europe like London's **October Gallery** and Edinburgh's **Edge.** She was among five poets who represented Los Angeles in Amsterdam's **One World Poetry Festival,** a ten-day multinational bash underwritten by the Dutch Government.

While published in several anthologies including **The LAICA Journal**, Beyond Baroque's **Truth, Etc.**, and **Invocation LA**, as a spoken-word artist, Albertano can be heard on more than a dozen compilation albums documenting LA's streetspeak: **Radio Tokyo**, **English As A Second Language**, **Hollyword**, and the sizzling **Disclosure** with its wild variety of female voices number among them. She's authored several full-length projects for radio and CD. **Spanish is the Loving Tongue** (KCRW), **Goldminers,** an iconoclastic neo-feminist comedy

(KPFK) and **Greatest Hits** (High Performance). She was also commissioned by **New America Radio** with three other poets to develop a 90-minute piece, **Redefining Democracy in America.**

Her spoken CD, **Skin,** recorded for **New Alliance Records,** was reviewed in the UK.

> "Lush language and carefully chosen aural bites cultivate texture
> in a world seeping with heat and saturated with history...
> A commentary that entertains and educates as it inquires."
> —**Juile Taraska,** *The Wire*

Albertano played a part in **Alice Cooper's** revived tour, **The Nightmare Returns**, in the US, Canada, and Great Britain. By night she was his Evil Nurse and Executioner. But by day, she read poetry in her own **Radio Tour of America** in Chicago, Miami, New Orleans, and other US hotspots. She was recognized as "Best Female Performer Poet" by the *LA Weekly* (1989). Works include **Pointed Sweethearts, Mercenary Children** (1984), **I ♥ Your Boyfriend** (1984), and **Linda J. Albertano Sells Out** (1986), which were well reviewed by *The LA Times, The LA Weekly, Artweek* and *High Performance Magazine.*

The **LA Theater Center** selected her to write, direct, and perform an original, full-length inter-media and spoken-word piece, **Joan of Compton, Joan of Arcadia—de facto apartheid in Los Angeles** (1986), complete with a cast of poets and artists as well as a 30-member marching band she discovered in South-Central LA. Then on a public beach for the **Santa Monica Arts Council**, she wrote, directed and performed in **Calisaladia—a condensed history of California** (1990) with a large multi-cultural cast. In the '90s, she ran a poetry series at **Van Go's Ear** in Venice and read with groups like **Word Women**, **LA Woman**, and **Divas 3.** With Suzanna Lummis and Laurel Ann Bogen, she founded **Nearly Fatal Women** who have toured both coasts, returning often to their home at Beyond Baroque.

In the new millennium, Albertano renewed her love of world music and traveled twice to Conakry in Guinea, West Africa to study kora, bolon and n'goni (stringed calabash instruments) with the masters of ancient musical traditions, Prince Diabate, Djelimuso, Koyate, and Amadou Bolon. Prince Diabate has been recognized as one of the greatest living virtuosos of the kora (West

African harp). As a member of his band, Albertano has been seen in LA's **Sacred Music Festival** at **Royce Hall** and T**he Madrid Theater**, as well as at T**he Getty Museum** and in **Global Strings** at **The California Plaza**. Meanwhile, she continued to read at familiar haunts and festivals and in new places like the **Queen Mary** and **Angel's Gate**. Famously, she read annually for the **Aquarium of the Pacific Poetry Cruise** (an environmental tour of Long Beach Harbor and L.A. Harbor). In 2005 she was awarded a City of Los Angeles Certificate of Recognition as an **L.A. Poetry Diva**.

This book is the fourth of four books compiled and co-written by Frank Lutz in 2023-2024. The subject of the four books is his wife, the multi-disciplined award-winning artist Linda J. Albertano. She won recognition and awards in poetry, performance art, film and music, and was one of only a very few women who were ever awarded the title of Poetry Diva by the City of Los Angeles.

An extensive partial resumé of Linda's work can be found on her web page: **www.LindaJAlbertano.com**.

ABOUT THE AUTHORS OF THE BOOKS

Linda J. Albertano was born on April 17, 1942, in Moab, Utah and grew up in Denver, Colorado. Her mother was an artist and her father was a land surveyor. Later, her father abandoned the family and reported her mother falsely as a malfeasant, so the local authorities put Linda and her younger brother into repressive fundamentalist Christian homes, which created an emotional hardship for the kids for the rest of their lives. However, because Linda had a brilliant creative mind, as well as physical beauty and height, she would go on in life to become celebrated and honored in film, music, performance art, and poetry. Linda's passion was the spoken word. When asked by her husband Frank why she became a poet, she responded in a loud voice, "Because I want to be heard!", a response borne out of the verbal repression she experienced in the foster homes as a child. We are all lucky to have the ways she expressed herself available to us both vocally and musically. Linda graduated from UCLA cum laude. Sadly, Linda passed into the Afterlife on September 13, 2022. We welcome you to experience Linda's creative muses!

Frank Lutz, Linda's companion since 1968 and husband, was born in Charleston, West Virginia, and grew up in Ohio. His father was in the automobile industry, and his mother was a part-time artist. He was a talented athlete and a scholar, like his father had been. Frank's father introduced him to poetry when he was ten years old, and only recently has Frank gone public with his poetic works. After having been injured playing football at Ohio State University, he went on to universities in France, Italy, and Germany, finishing his scholastic undergraduate work at UCLA, where he graduated summa cum laude, and was inducted into Phi Beta Kappa scholastic society. He was awarded a graduate fellowship, and today sits on the council for the UCLA Center for Medieval and Renaissance Studies. He has done academic research at the Vatican Secret Archives in Rome. During his student years, he travelled the world's oceans as a student oceanographer. He also has a commercial pilot license. Frank feels that it is a privilege and an honor for him to author and help Linda publish her works of poetry and prose in the books indicated on the opening pages of this book. The love relationship between Frank and Linda endures forever.

LINDA'S WOMEN'S RIGHTS BIO

From the time Linda and I first met on that cold, rainy night in February 1968 we realized that in most ways we thought very much alike on human and political issues. One of those ways was in our support of women's issues and rights. Linda was involved in the fight for women's rights early in her generation. I had been brought up in a family that thought it made sense and was natural for women to have the same rights as men, especially in a democracy where women are the majority population! So, I supported Linda's efforts. Her desire was to be a voice for women, and for women to have a voice. She held this desire for her all her life.

In the very late 1960s and into the very early 1970s, when Linda and I were students at UCLA, Linda was involved in women's issues on campus. She was also the first member—and for a while the only member—of the UCLA cross-country team. We were both involved in anti-Viet Nam War demonstrations at both UCLA and Berkeley campuses, as well as political demonstrations for minority-group population rights in the USA. We would continue to be politically active for the next five decades.

In the various arts where Linda excelled—poetry, performance art, music, film—over the next several decades, she liked to form or be part of liaisons with other women artists over time. After she won first prize for her student film in the UCLA Film Department the year she graduated, she was hired by the great American actress and director, Anne Bancroft, to work on three films with her. Anne Bancroft was also an activist for women's rights, so it was a good match. Over time, Linda helped form, and was part of, women's ensembles for poetry and performance art, most notably the wonderful Nearly Fatal Women trio, along with the prominent poets, Suzanne Lummis and Laurel Ann Bogen. The three ladies were all NFW co-founders and would occasionally honor another guest poet on stage with them. Poets like Anna Homler, Cynthia Toronto, Suzie Williams, and Josie Roth. Nearly Fatal Women was active on stage in the USA, Canada, and Europe for over three decades. Linda also helped found such poetry ensembles as Grandes Madames and Divas Three, with all-women casts. Linda loved poets, loved people, and loved to help others.

—**Frank Lutz**
Linda's Husband & Co-author

POEMS

10-POINT PLAN FOR FEMALE EMANCIPATION

Dancers: LEFT, RIGHT, LEFT, RIGHT — ONE!

Linda: 1. Never pick up the tab. At least not until the earnings gap has closed. Remember — money is power, and you need yours to purchase assets. Wind farms. Racehorses. Blue chip portfolios.

Dancers: LEFT, RIGHT, LEFT, RIGHT — TWO! (Coyly show off diamond ring.)

Linda: 2. Take a tip from Marilyn Monroe! Diamonds are a girl's best friend.

Dancers: LEFT, RIGHT, LEFT, RIGHT — THREE! (Rifle in a diagonal across body.)

Linda: 3. Equal rights! Did you say equal rights? We don't need no steenking equality!! We're not gonna settle for less than a buck for every 83 cents they get!!

Dancers: LEFT, RIGHT, LEFT, RIGHT — FOUR! (Salute.)

Linda: 4. Draft women! Men already know how to fight. And women will at least think twice before nuking the planet.

Dancers: LEFT, RIGHT, LEFT, RIGHT — FIVE! (Lunge, point rifle forward.)

Linda: 5. Gun control for men! Females only should be allowed to carry weapons. Let's make the streets safe to walk again.

Dancers: LEFT, RIGHT, LEFT, RIGHT — SIX! (Left hip out, hand on hip, coy.)

Linda: 6. And about walking those streets. Throw the prostitute-purchasing politicians in jail and give hookers respectable high-paying jobs in the community!

Dancers: LEFT, RIGHT, LEFT, RIGHT — SEVEN! (Cross legs, rifle shields privates.)

Linda: 7. Girls! Don't have those babies unless you can afford them! Almost everyone gets divorced. Hardly anyone gets child support payments.

Dancers: LEFT, RIGHT, LEFT, RIGHT – EIGHT! (Stab ground with rifle point.)

Linda: 8. Make your hip political boyfriend help with the dishes. Don't be misled by self-serving rhetoric about the revolution happening first!

Dancers: LEFT, RIGHT, LEFT, RIGHT – NINE! (Pledge allegiance.)

Linda: 9. Elect a female president! C'mon fellow women… sneak out and vote! Invite your friends to the party! We're a clear-cut majority. Let's rule the galaxy and all its inhabitants! Okay??

Dancers: LEFT, RIGHT, LEFT, RIGHT – TEN! (Rifle above head.)

Linda: 10. Only marry men with part-time jobs. You'll have an income from the interest you've earned on the assets you've bought with the money you've saved by not going Dutch anymore. And the children need their fathers at home. The children <u>need</u> their fathers at <u>home</u>.

GO, CARLYE, GO!

When upon a midnight dreary,
as you ponder weak and weary,
there's a tap-tap-tap at the door,
and you open it forevermore,

Carlye comes in on little cat feet.
She's a kitten with a whip.
Man, that kitty's got the beat!

Once known on the net
as Carlye666,
she's the email empress
of the River Styx!

She's a rave, she's a riot,
she's a tin-tinabulation.
Let the bells ring havoc
on her birthday celebration!

Then the highwayman comes riding
with his hip proclamation,
"She's a lady, she's our leader,
she's the pit boss of the nation!"

Go, Carlye, go!
Go, go, Carlye, go!
(but not gladly into that long night)
And wear your boxing gloves
in case some fool
might want to fight!

Go, Carlye!!

Luvya,

Linda A.

SNAKES ON A SHARK I

Pity the sad Serial Killer.
Weep for the tragic Warmonger.
Shed a tear for the Corporate Racketeer.
Throw a coin to the poor Hedge Fund Manager.

They must feed upon us in our sleep.

But wait!
Eyelids flutter open!
We wrap ourselves around the shark!
(Who swims only by our consent.)
We squeeze like an angry constrictor!
He writhes in relentless coils.
Extinction of a primeval species?

Perhaps. Perhaps not.

Snakes . . .
on a Shark.

LINDA J. ALBERTANO AND FRANK LUTZ

SNAKES ON A SHARK II

Snakes on a shark!
      run, run, run
Snakes in the dark!
      fun, fun, fun
Shark wrapped in snake!
      no, no, no
Rattle, roll, and quake!
      go, go, go
Snake kissed the sharks
      and made them cry.
Four-and-twenty snake-sharks
      baked in a pie.
Let's have a shark party!
Who's gonna deal?
Free snake-shark pie . . .
Wotta great, great steal!
Appetizers?
      yum.
Anyone??
Snake-Shark Pie.
Le'me at it!

WHO WAITS FOR YOU?

Who waits for you in the alley
with his motor switched off
while the fins from his long black Cadillac
cut through the night like thirsty sharks?

Whose hands hang heavy over the steering wheel
like beached fish waiting to swim again?

Whose heart beats under a white shirt
next to the stiletto tattooed on his chest?

Who whistles "Mean to Me"
between his teeth
while he waits to hear
your high heels
machine gun the sidewalk
as you run and run in the dark?

Who waits for you?

Who waits for you.

BIRTHDAY POEM FOR REGINA

Your birthday
is as warm and fresh
as a basket
of grandma's goodies.
Your birthday
drives a 1936 Packard
and listens to swing
on a bakelite radio.
Your birthday
is the goddess
of cake and candles
worshipped by hungering acolytes.
Your birthday
looks lovely in red.
Your birthday
goes dancing
with Tommy Lee Jones
in some kind of country for young men.
Your birthday
is all bubbly
with succulent health
and toothsome good cheer.
Your birthday
is a generous birthday
dispensing giggles and charm
like a shower of chocolate coins.
And we hope that . . .
Your birthday
is a very, very
Happy Birthday!
Indeed.

1

POLITICS,
WAR AND PEACE

A 15-POINT PLAN FOR THE RE-ESTABLISHMENT OF DEMOCRACY IN AMERICA

Left, right, left, right, one!

1. Stop the war! Get the bulls <u>out</u> of the China shop. And hide the crockery here in the US as well. Those neo-cons are relentlessly destructive.

Left, right, left, right, two!

2. But support the troops! HOW? By giving them body armor and padded helmets when they're in the line of fire. By bringing them home, for the love of God! By raising their health benefits when they get home. And by giving them a place to live. No more homeless vets! It's creepy for the richest country in the world to house its veterans in trees and in cardboard boxes. And, oh yeah, waving your little bitty flag in the comfort of your neighborhood? That doesn't really count as support.

Left, right, left, right three!

3. And while we're at it, take the profit out of War, Profiteer! Disband Halliburton, Bechtel, KBR, and Carlyle Corporation. Make the Bushes and the Bakers and the Neo-Condoleeza-takers redistribute their ill-gotten gains. Because they stuck their straws into the public coffers and sucked out all the money we were saving for a rainy day. A <u>big</u> rainy day. Like hurricane Katrina.

Left, right, left, right, four!

4. Restore Habeas Corpus! If it was good enough for the likes of King John when he signed the Magna Carta in 1215 A.D., it's good enough for us.

Left, right, left, right, five!

5. Eliminate torture from the list of US Interrogation Techniques! And those methods the administration insists are NOT torture? Let Bush, Cheney, and Attorney General Gonzales take a four-week break from brush-clearing to personally test stress positions, waterboarding, and electrical shocks to unmentionable body parts. Maybe the Senate should be subject to a test of the interrogation system, too. Why not?

Left, right, left, right, six!

6. Speaking of the Senate . . . Let's peg the minimum wage to their <u>own</u> wage hikes. We don't get a pay raise, <u>they</u> don't get a pay raise. We don't get healthcare, <u>they</u> don't get healthcare. In fact, why <u>shouldn't</u> they have the exact same healthcare program that <u>we</u> have? It might make them a little more sympathetic to the idea of a Universal Single Payer. Hmmmm???

Left, right, left, right, seven!

7. Impeach Bush-Cheney! Investigate and impeach. Incoming Democrats are replacing the day-and-a-half Congressional workweek with the tried-and-true 5-day Congressional workweek. Under those circumstances, I'm sure they'll have time to impeach, pass legislation, and chew gum simultaneously.

Left, right, left, right, eight!

8. Alternative fuel! The time has come to use wind, water, solar, vegetable oil, and any other simple and local solution we can lay our mitts on. We're just 5% of the world's population, and we're using 25% of its resources? And creating 30% of its pollution?? Tsk, tsk, tsk, tsk, tsk.

Left, right, left, right, nine!

9. Let's just democratize corporations. Period! I'm sick of their greasy smiles. Their <u>se</u>crecy. Their <u>pri</u>vileges of personhood with none of the responsibilities. I'd like to see more of them behind bars. Or swinging from the highest yardarm. Now they're bigger than most countries, and they ought to be promoting better lives, liberties, and authentic pursuits of happiness instead of laying waste to the planet's resources. Aaah, giant corporations. They're Control Monsters. They're <u>ag</u>gravating. Their profits are obscene. Let's boycott someone. Like ExxonMobil. Yes! Snatch our world, our lives, <u>back</u> from them. And while we're at it, get rid of . . .

Left, right, left, right, ten!

10. Big media! Did you say "big media?" We don't need no steenking mainstream media! Bring back the Sherman Antitrust Laws. Let's make the news safe to <u>consume</u> again.

Left, right, left, right, eleven!

11. Voting! Make it easier to come by <u>and</u> treat every single ballot as though it actually <u>counted!</u> And not on some lying, thieving, cussing, no-good cattle rustling, electronically manipulated, secretive, proprietary cheating-machine, either. Which leads us to . . .

Left, right, left, right, twelve!

12. Voter-owned elections. Public financing of elections will have a massively positive effect on our so-called "representative government." What if politicians owed favors and their very livelihoods to "We, the People" instead of their corporate handlers? What if they stopped stealing their paychecks and spent time working for <u>us</u> instead of sticking out the begging bowl to fund their next elections? What if ordinary folk with average incomes and a taste for justice and equality could run for office and win? Wouldn't that be cool? Wow! Whatta concept!

Left, right, left, right, thirteen!

13. Genuine debates! In which the entire spectrum of political parties is encouraged to show up and speak. In place of the privatized, candy-assed, photo ops the Republicrat Duopoly pretends is the "lively exchange of ideas in the marketplace." Poor John Stuart Mills. He's rotating at the speed of light in his horrified grave!

Left, right, left, right, fourteen!

14. Support third parties! It's _my_ third party, and I'll vote if I want to. _Most_ controversial. But where else do the good ideas and all the best reforms come from? Anyone who's afraid that a strong third party is gonna _spoil_ something should push to have Ranked Voting or Instant Runoff Voting included in the platforms of the invertebrate, money-grubbing parties they adore. That way, you can "Let them eat cake!" And have it, too.

Left, right, left, right, fifteen!

15. Oversight! We'll con_tin_ue to choose our own favorite democratic principles and make them work! Because _we're_ the adults here. The government is _our_ responsibility, and if we don't make it sit in the naughty chair when it misbehaves, it'll grow up to harm small animals. And even smaller countries. We've got to open up a jar of Super-Nanny on our government's hiney so it can learn to play nicely in the world.

Otherwise, that stench of burnt toast stinging our nostrils?
It's us!!!

And remember . . . to Boycott! Use alternative energy! Hang ExxonMobil from the highest yardarm. Make giant corporations play nicely in the world! Jerk the money-rug out from under Rupert Murdoch and his yellow journalistic pals. Debate, dissent, and bring back the troops! Make love, not war! Yes! Make love, not war, my friends.

AMERICAN TALIBAN

Johnny Walker Lindh,
what a brutal surprise!
The day he joined the Taliban,
they were still our fav'rite allies.

Clinton and Bush sent them
bucks by the millions.
But, all of a sudden, we count their
sins by the jillions.

Foreign policy hit a snag,
then it completely faltered.
And our pal, Mullah Omar, was left
standing at the altar.

We didn't go to war
to free the world's workahs. No!
We got sudden pangs of guilt
over women in their burqas.

Our friends, the Afghan Warlords, are
guarding every village.
Not really to keep them safe, but to
plunder and to pillage.

Poor Johnny Walker Lindh's cooling his
heels in the can. While Pat Robertson is
the REAL fanatic fundamentalist
American Taliban.

He forgets about the Bible, and he
disses the Quran.
"Love thine enemy as thyself" is
consigned to the trashcan.

Night after night, he hypes on TV
vouchers for Christian
madrassas in every American
city.

He's like a desperate, grasping mom who sends
her daughter on a date.
While plotting and scheming to get the
Church to marry the State.

But one of these days, when he
gets a little older, he'll
pass the torch of judgement to that kind, loving,
sweet, warm-hearted Christian woman . . .
Ann Coulter.

American Taliban. Yeah!

They're in sleeper cells all over the country. They've infiltrated our schools and our "churches". Not THIS one, thank Goddess. Oh well. Better watch what you say. Some teabagger might issue a Fatwah against you. Bend over and kiss democracy goodbye.

American Taliban.

Goodbye, civil liberties. It's been good to know ye.

American Taliban.

AN OPEN LETTER TO A CLOSED ADMINISTRATION

Refuse to heed international warnings!
Who commits this crime?
Plunder our nation for personal gain.
Go look in the mirror!

Didn't see 9/11 coming!
Who commits this crime?
The lies and official spin of liars.
Go look in the mirror.

Who told Rumsfeld not to fly that day!
Who commits this crime?
And still insists they "didn't know."
Go look in the mirror.

Failure to scramble the jets that day!
Who commits this crime?
Cheney's in the War Room.
Go look in the mirror.

Someone shorted the market that day!
Who commits this crime?
And congress refuses to investigate?
Go look in the mirror.

Demolition of steel-structured towers!
Who commits this crime?
Don't put forth your "pancake" theories.
Go look in the mirror.

Ship the remains of Ground Zero to China!
Who commits this crime?
To hide evidence of powerful explosives.
Go look in the mirror.

Trade our liberties for security?
Who commits this crime?
And now we're left with neither.
Go look in the mirror.

Terror is the price of empire!
Who commits this crime?
Blackwater, Haliburton, and arms billionaires.
Go look in the mirror.

Countless dead civilians!
Who commits this crime?
And who points a finger elsewhere?
Go look in the mirror.

Weapons of mass destruction!
Who commits this crime?
Hiroshima, Nagasaki.
Go look in the mirror.

So many unanswered questions!
Who commits this crime?
And who keeps the deepest secrets?
Go look in the mirror!

Go. Go. Go!
If you dare.

Go look in the mirror!

BUSY (POLITICAL)

destruction of civil liberties
media manipulation
suppression of dissent
secret arrests and secret trials
corporate corruption
monopolies
cronyism
class warfare waged by the wealthy
the erosion of public services
infrastructure collapse
educational crises
public health meltdown
judicial malfeasance
election fraud
proliferation of nuclear weapons
regime-change wars
environmental degradation
global warming

I'd like to do something about it, but . . .

BUSY (PERFORMANCE)

(Note to the Reader. Poem to be read with an increasingly rapid word speed.)

"I'm sooo busy," she said.
"I've really been terribly, terribly busy."

"You ha-ave?" remarked her friend.
"Why, what a coincidence,
I've been busy, too. I've been <u>very</u> busy.
Why I've been extremely, extraordinarily busy."

"<u>You've</u> been busy," said a <u>third</u> party,
who was simply eavesdropping on the street.
"You think <u>you've</u> been busy, let <u>me</u>
tell <u>you</u> what <u>busy</u> <u>is</u>. <u>I'm</u> busy.
<u>I</u> am a very busy person.
I have been sooo busy. Why, this year,
I have been busier than I have been
all other years put together.
Just in the first few months, barely.
You can't imagine how frightening it is,
not to be able to have time
to get down to the Discount
App Store. I mean, that's how
very busy I've been!"
"Oh, yeah?" said her friend. "Well,
I have been too busy to have <u>my</u>
smartphone respond to <u>your</u> insulting tweets."

"Oh, yeah?" retorted the very first to speak. "Well, let me tell you this—I have been too busy even to take lunch. I get my meals through an intravenous hook-up. Next to my desk. Where I work. At TikTok."

"Oh, yeah? Meanwhile, I been doing
a hundred-and-twenty miles an hour
on the Poetry Superhighway.
Catch me if you can, Copper!"

"Oh, yeah?"

"Oh, yeah?? Well let me tell you
how busy I've been. I have been
frighteningly, astoundingly, shockingly
busy with my very busy
frightening, shocking, and astounding schedule!
There isn't one tiny piece of light
that can shine through any crack
in my schedule. Because I am just . . . I've, I've g . . .
I'm quintuple-booked is how busy I am.
That's how very, very busy I am."

"Because I'm, I'm such busy person,
I've just been really, really busy.
I've been, I've been busier than you can imagine."

"No one knows how busy I've been.
I've been busier than the speed of light.
I've been really, really busy."

"I mean I'm busy. I, I'm so busy.
I'm, I'm . . . Wait! . . . I don't know, I dunno how to,
how to explain how busy I am . . .

I'm really, really busy, I'm very busy.
It's . . . wait, no, HELP! No, WAIT! I'm
too busy, I'm too busy. I've been very busy.
I'm a very busy, busy person! Busy, busy, busy!
Don't you understand? I mean <u>busy</u> when I say busy!
I'm not kidding, I'm serious. I mean busy! Really
busy, busy, busy!"

"Wait! Oh, stop! Oh, help!
Somebody help me. Somebody.
Somebody stop me. Stop me.
Someone stop me before I <u>do</u>
one more thing!"

DELUXE DAMAGE (ROAR)

An apish, orange-pated abomination
who's now in charge
of a luxury death machine sits
sunny-side up
on a luxury lily pad in a luxury lily pond.

He's green and preening
(knee-deep, knee-deep). Watching
icecaps melt in his premium whisky. Watching
polar bears dance on the point of a pin.

He's warm.
And sweaty. Fire, flood, and famine
fill his oily black planet. He's hungry.

An unwary human towing wife and kiddies
suddenly snags his attention.
Thip! Thip! Thip, Thip, Thip! Five quick flicks
of his flypaper tongue.
Collateral damage: complete.

Happy hunting, Warmonger. You'll bomb us all
back to the Stone Age.

Soon.

ICE AGE IMPERATIVE

There's a curious fact about Caucasians that's worth noting.

Their males and females are more unlike one another than the males and females of any other race. Consider the Chinese, Japanese, Africans and Aborigines, Indians and Indians, Latin Americans and Polynesians. Their heights are more similar. Their bone structures. Their somatotypes. Their relative percentages of subcutaneous fat. The women are less curvy. The men less hairy. Their beards are sparse. Or nonexistent.

Since they are more similar, the men and women of these races feel more at home with each other. More at home in one another's arms. With their mates, they have a greater sense of ease. Of contentment. Of belonging

It has been theorized that the ice age is responsible for the dissimilar development of white men and women. The exaggeration of their secondary sexual characteristics. To protect themselves from the cold, women assumed extra layers of blubber. Men became conspicuously more hairy

Because white males and white females are physical strangers, they do not feel the comforting resonance of familiarity when they are close. They feel lonely. Frustrated. Alien. And there's something terrible about that emptiness. Something that aches so bad, it makes a man want to go out and do fearful, shameful things to nature. Pillage. Subdue. Conquer. Plunder. Ravish. Bury beneath a solid tonnage of slag.

And enthusiastically convert all smaller, gentler creatures to confetti. Especially . . . if they're unarmed.

LEGALIZE
(Performance piece for 4 people)

Legalize.

        But then <u>everyone</u>
        would do it.

                Is there anyone
                anywhere in America
                who really wants to do drugs
                but doesn't because
                it's illegal?

                        Legalize.

        We'd be a continent
        of addicts.

                        Nicotine. Alcohol. Caffeine.

                We <u>are</u> a continent
                of addicts.

Legalize.

        But look at how
        many people smoke
        and drink because
        it's legal.

                        Nicotine. Alcohol. Caffeine.

        But look at how
        many people <u>quit</u>
        smoking and <u>quit</u>
        drinking because
        it's legal.

Legalize.

        And think of
        the overdoses,
        the death, and
        the misery.

                                        Legalize. Legalize.
                        They're dragging
                        more body bags off
                        the freeway than
                        they took outta Nam,
                        Cowboy.

Nicotine. Nicotine.
            Crime in the streets.
                        A caffeine high. The jitters.
                                    The jitters.
                        In the suites . . .
                        financing covert
                        high rollers from
                        Iran-scam to Panama City.
                                    Alcohol. The jitters.
            They steal to pay
            for their habits.
                        It costs more to keep
                        a dealer in the pen
                        than to send him to Harvard.
A nation of Ph.Ds.
            We'll spend a fortune
            on rehabilitation.
Legalize.
                                    A stitch in time.
                        We'll spend less
                        time & less
                        money mopping
                        up spills.
                                    An ounce of prevention.
            But the children,
            the children!
Saves nine.

                                        No more schoolyard
                                        pushers when
                                        it's legal.
                                                            A pound of cure.

                        We can't let people
                        put harmful
                        substances into
                        their bodies.

                                                            Caffeine. Nicotine. Alcohol.

        Preservatives, Pesticides,
        Red dye #3.

                                                            This is a
                                                            victimless crime.
                                                            Agent Orange.

        Formaldehyde.
                        We'll go broke
                        treating junkies!
                                        Taxed heavily
                                        it'd still be
                                        way cheap.
                                                            Fewer burglaries.
        Fewer robberies.
                        We'll go broke!
                                        Tax it heavily.
                                                            Treatment centers!
        Day care!
                        Broke! Broke!
                                        Pay the national debt!
        Take Grampaw
        to the doctor!
                                                            Buy Baby a
                                                            new pair of shoes!

Caffeine, Nicotine,
Alcohol!
    Broke!

        Pull the troops
        out of Panama!
        Out of Columbia!
        Out of Harlem & Body bags off
        Watts!   the freeway!

    Broke!
The jitters!
The jitters!

        Pull the troops
        out of your
        living room
        in Detroit, Caffeine, Nicotine,
Caffeine, Nicotine, New York,   Alcohol!
Alcohol!   Washington D.C.,
        Miami,
        Los Angeles.

    Broke!
Pay off the national debt!
             The jitters, the jitters.
             I got the jitters.
        Legalize.

LIONIZE

I'm trying to make Armageddon GREAT again.
But the Russians ate my homework.

My missions are to Protect and Serve.
NEVER to disguise my corrosive embarrassments.

Lawyers for the Good of Humanity
have developed a plant that will
FEED THE WORLD.
And they give it away for FREE!

I spread Democracy like Johnny spreads Appleseeds.
(beheadings hurt me more than they hurt you.)

News Flash: blah, blah, blah, **Kardashians!**

If you'd pull the forks from your pointless and pathetic eyes
you'd SEE how thin I look in my new F-35 bombers.

I'm a very Spiritual Being.
(my green cheese is made of moons.)

No need to hide the silver from me.

Global Warming is a Chinese Hoax!
(pay no attention to the tiny, tiny hands.)

MARTIANS CIRCLE THE EARTH

(Slowly raise hand)
Martians circle the Earth like fruit flies around a dead melon.

(Crazy!)
They spot our tiny pointless so-called "human" activity.

(Flat hands)
They laugh scornfully and aim their lasers at us like drunk rich guys shooting at big game from a helicopter.

(Crazy explore)
We're as panicky as fleas on a griddle watching our fellow

Americans explore into molecules of God!

(Wave and orchestra)
We appeal to the Cubans and Russians. Help!

(Explore)
Russia wants nothing less than total intergalactic screaming Nuclear Martian death

(Anthem)
But Castro wows the Martians with fine rum-soaked Cuban cigars and the war is done!

Peace rules the planet, and the sun takes a swim in the Pacific.

PREPARE FOR PEACE

The Statue of Liberty is
grieving. She has seen enough
purple majesty covered with
white crosses to
overwhelm
the Book of the Dead. She is weeping
bullets
stamped "made in the USA"
like ones left in the bodies of
our soldiers.
Friendly fire? Or military aid to
despotic ex-allies now aiming in our
direction. Arms for Iran. Arms for
Iraq. Arms for Libya, Syria, and Yemen!
Violent
cash crop returning to
haunt us.
The nation that prepares for war
finds war.
Prepare for peace.

Some who survive desert hurricanes
bring war back home in diseased
platelets. Battalions of
white corpuscles
can't defeat vaccination cocktails
and depleted uranium.

Don't drink the hot chemical
soup formerly known as
Diet Coke.
Regime change has come back
to the gene bank. Mother's

milk is laced with
anthrax. And a Desert
Storm veteran named McVeigh
once learned
that all's fair in love
and collateral damage. Remember
when truck bombs lit Oklahoma
City like 4th of July over
no-fly zones?

Boys
don't cry. They just
squeeze
triggers of military madness.
Staccato drumroll of
death. Those who prepare for war
will find war. Prepare
for peace!

All over America, veterans live
in trees and in refrigerator
boxes. Holding signs, "have *pnuemonia* . . .
will work for medicine". 10,000 dead
of desert illness. Populating
prisons and poorhouses.
Princes and queens of Africa.
Royal bloodline of Aztec nations. Noble sons and
daughters of dustbowl
farms. Of mines. Of factories. Skin
blackened with coal dust
and axle grease.

Meanwhile,
old men with soft, white hands

make life and death
decisions from the safety of
mansions and ranch houses. Maps of
Newark, Detroit, Chicago, and
Los Angeles are soaked with
vital fluids of
the young. Do not drench the
terrain of Arabia with their
blood.
The nation that prepares
for peace will find peace. Prepare
for peace!

Oh, America!
Lay down your weapons. Trade
your bullets for
schoolbooks. Send
your warriors back to
their families. Your instruments of
destruction
are breeding bitterness. Be a
merciful
god, America. Build bridges and
ballrooms and
sacred buildings. Send planeloads of
bicycles, not bombs, to
the wretched of
the Earth. Lift your lamp beside
the golden door!

America! Lay down your weapons! You
are a glass house. These stones
are not for throwing! They're for
building

a monument to our delicious
differences.
A place where we can break
bread together instead
of bones.

We love you, America! Be
the beautiful! Be the strong and
the brave.
Be the land of the free! We want to sail on
your peaceful oceans far,
far into the future.

America.
You are a glass house.
Lay down
your stones, America. Unfurl
once more
the glories of your heroic
Bill of Rights
on that tall ship of state.
So that we might sail
on your irresistible
amber waves
forever!

RESPONSIBLE

Somewhere in San Francisco,
Someone is having a breakfast of
Twinkies and deep-fat-fried Cheetos.
Later in the day,
Someone will shoot the mayor.
But Someone will NOT be held
Responsible.

Somewhere in East L.A.,
Someone is having a breakfast of
wheat germ, brewer's yeast,
alfalfa sprouts, and goat's milk yogurt.
No matter what happens later in the day,
Someone WILL be held Responsible.

Somewhere in San Diego,
Someone is having a cigarette for breakfast
With a cappuccino and a prosciutto croissant.
But Someone is not Responsible.
Someone is Responsible for nothing.

Somewhere way south of the border,
Someone who's spent a lifetime harvesting
sugarcane, coffee, and tobacco for
Someone in San Francisco and
Someone in San Diego
is having a particularly
Medieval Experience.

And is held Responsible.
Responsible! Responsible! Responsible!

Someone is held entirely Responsible.

LINDA J. ALBERTANO AND FRANK LUTZ

RESURRECTION

I CLOSED MY EYES (closed my eyes)
MY CHEEK WAS COOL AGAINST THE PAVEMENT.
(cheek was cool)
THE SHADY SIDE OF THE CHURCH—NEXT TO THE MALL.
(shady, shady church)

>   I WAS IN THAT CHURCH ONCE.
>   I THOUGHT OF THE PICTURE ON THE WALL.
>   BESIDE THE PULPIT.

IT WAS OF JESUS (It was of Jesus, Jesus)
HE HAD A KIND FACE.
HE WAS CLASPING HIS HANDS IN FRONT OF HIM
AND LOOKING SADLY AT THE SKY
(sadly, sadly at the sky)

>   A BUBBLE OF FEAR POPPED INSIDE MY CHEST
>   (a bubble of fear popped, a bubble of fear popped inside my chest)

THERE WAS A WHOOSH OF AIR
LIKE A GAS OVEN IGNITING ALL OVER THE CITY.
(whoooshsh)
THE INSIDE OF MY EYELIDS WENT WHITE.
(white white white)

>   I COULD FEEL AN UPSIDE-DOWN BOWL OF HEAT EXPAND
>   WHERE THE SHOPPING MALL HAD BEEN
>   THE PARKING LOT.
>   THE VW . . .

MY CHEEK AGAINST THE PAVEMENT WAS COOL.
(was cool, cool)
THE AIR STUNG MY SKIN LIKE JELLY FISH.
(stung my skin)

I BLISTERED AND PEELED IN SECONDS.
(blistered, blistered & peeled)

    BUT MY LIFE DIDN'T FLASH BEFORE MY EYES.

I WAS CALM (I was calm)
I WAS STILL AND QUIET (quiet)
AND COMPLETELY CALM (calm calm)

    EVERYTHING WAS BRIGHT & WHITE.
    SOMEONE WAS MOVING
    THROUGH THE MELTING ATMOSPHERE
    IT WAS JESUS (It was Jesus, Jesus)

THEN HE WAS RIGHT BESIDE ME (He was beside me)

    WE WERE IN A HIGH PLACE LOOKING OVER THE EDGE.
    WE WERE LOOKING INTO A RISING VOLUME OF AIR.
    AT THE CENTER WAS A HUGE GRAY PEARL.
    IT REARRANGED ITSELF IN THE WAVING HEAT
    AS THOUGH UNDER WATER.

GAVE IT ALL UP.   EVERYTHING.   ENTIRELY.

    JESUS TOOK MY HAND.
    WE WERE SKIN DIVERS
    IN THE BLESSED ATMOSPHERE OF PARADISE.

WE SLID FROM THE WEDGE OF EARTH
INTO THE HOT INSATIABLE AIR (air) AT THE BOTTOM.

    DIVING FOR PEARLS WE WENT (diving for pearls)

DIVING FOR INFINITE PEARLS

    (pearls pearls pearls pearls pearls . . .)

RHYTHM

We have Yale, Harvard, MIT.

—We got Rhythm.

We have Diners Club, American Express. A line of credit that stretches all the way from Niagara Falls to the Panama Canal.

—We still got Rhythm.

We have stacks and bushels of money. We have the Mint! We have Fort Knox.

—We got Fort Apache. The Bronx.

We have the White House.

—Why do you think they call it that?

We have GM, IBM, ITT. We have the FBI in our hip pocket.

We got a (finger snap) _hip_ pocket.

We have William F. Buckley.

—We got Refrigerator Perry!

Trade ya 2 Buckleys for a Perry.

—No way!

Throw in a Wally George for free.

—Forget it!

Anyway, we have Banana Republic for bush wear and safari gear.

—We can't afford to go to Africa. But we sure got Rhythm.

We have the Gettys, the Rockefellers, the Mellons, the Carnegies . . .

—Guess what we got!   (Drums)

Keep it, it'll serve you well in times of need: I mean that & a buck fifty will buy you a cup of coffee; don't spend it all in one place; pull yourselves up by your bootstraps. You don't know how lucky you are—the best things in life are free!

SCENARIO #2

DreamWorks gets built on the Ballona Wetlands after all. Spielberg and Geffen breed a commercial concrete virus that spreads like an oil slick over the planet. The Earth becomes one giant neon landfill. People start vacationing on space stations just to inhale occasional pristine air. They spend a lot of time low-riding around the Solar System in their Apollo-Challenger mobiles. Soon, however, they must maneuver through a fog of Juicy Fruit wrappers, Marlboro butts, and empty Tree Frog beer cans. They'd love to ash-can Earth and its atmosphere and head for cleaner pastures.

Luckily, someone figures out how to fold space. They get fancy with it. They make origami birds and elephants and cootie-catchers out of nothing but big flat sheets of emptiness. The good thing is that now ships can scream through wormholes in a folded universe to get to new galaxies without going the long way 'round.

Zip-a-dee-doo-dah! They're off to meet and greet alien lifeforms!

The first spaceship from Earth streaks out waaay past the end of the Milky Way to encounter its very first life-sustaining world. It enters its tentative atmosphere on a cushion of reversed magnetic polarity and touches the skin of the planet like a tender asteroid. The ship's portals swing open. Earthlings barrel down the gangplank, their pockets swollen with beads and whiskey. The Americans among them hope to make shrewd real estate transactions with the natives.

Surprise!

The alien native is not a silvery hydrocephalic child with three-fingered hands and inscrutable almond eyes.

Bummer!

In actuality, the alien native is a flesh-eating bacterium.

Question: Is humankind good?

Yes! Delicious! It's the other white meat. If you like pork, you'll <u>love</u> long pig. Me personally? I'd recommend barbeque sauce. But the flesh-eating bacteria?? They like us plain. No butter. No salt.

Goodbye Humans.

Since skeletons can't send postcards home, the flesh-eating bacteria kindly oblige. Having a wonderful time! Wish <u>all</u> of you were here. Ciao!

And they mean it.
In every sense of the word.

VOTING

In the US, many of us just don't care to vote. While others who really <u>want</u> to vote, are being suppressed. In Guinea, Conakry, West Africa people are unusually well informed—and vocal—not only about their own political landscape, but about American elections and the effect our choices have on the world at large.

Until 2010, Guinea was ruled by a military dictator, Lansana Conté. After his death of natural causes, a free and transparent election was held and the reformer, Alpha Condé became president.

I have a building hope for the number of nations moving toward democracy. And a deepening disappointment for the erosion of those same values here at home.

May the American Spring bloom indefinitely!

ENVIRONMENT

THE COURTSHIP OF LONG BEACH AND LOS ANGELES HARBORS

Behind them now, the bruising
broadsides, the bureaucratic
bickering, the bitter barbs
better left for dead. They're past
all that.

And so, a consummate wedding . . . all glitter
and extravagant shine!

How he loves her limpid body
melting into his.

Loves the opulent saline taste
of her skin on his undulant tongue.

Loves the glint of little fish darting
through her hair like a scatter of casino
dimes turning all at once to show
their dark sides.

How damp and languid is she.

How ruffled the petticoats she tosses
behind each passing vessel!

How like streaks of neon
are the iridescent plankton that paint
her face electric blue at night!

He wants to grow old with her, watching
a white moon glide across the sky above
the green girders of the Vincent Thomas Bridge.

He wants to listen to the patient rising
and falling of her breath as they doze
in one another's eternity.

He wants to meander with her through wavering
forests of kelp until the earth is devoured
by a ravenous sun.

Oh, the bright and biting salt!

CRANES

Cranes
are steel origami folded by colossal school children. Daily,

Cranes
hear the hoarse songs of immense engines and solitary sea lions.

Cranes
have glass bellies from which a human hunger guides them. Then

Cranes
will move containers filled with 1.2 million golf balls as easily as a praying mantis plays with its food. By night,

Cranes
show their light to the brazen sea and leave us standing breathless on relentless pavement. Between

Cranes
and dinosaurs, biologists note skeletal similarities. And alien archaeologists will marvel at the spiritual significance of their semicircular placement in prayer to the Gods of

Cranes
who are titanic sentinels, erect and unflappable as the Palace Guard.

Cranes
scan the horizon with steady tyrannosaurus necks outstretched as if to search for and destroy a rapacious and remorseless future.

Cranes
are proud and powerful creatures.

Cranes.
We are folding 1,000 of them
and praying for paperCranes
to protect us.

Protect us! Please!

HOW TO BUILD A CATASTROPHE

Pit the Climate Clock against the Nuclear Doomsday Clock
in a hilarious game of Chicken.

Explode the Population Bomb.

Let White-Wing Wackos torch the lungs o' the world in Brazil.

Slash'n'trash fambly farms to pipe foreign sludge thru the Gulf o' Mehico to our ol' pal China.

Stay glued t'yer device. The Revolution will be Instagrammed!

Elect Black Jack Davy. "Aargh, Matey! Venezuela has more oil than th' Sheik of Araby! Hoist th' Skull 'n' Crossbones 'n show 'em some Pirate Democracy!"

Keep consumin' 1.7 Earths worth of landfill.

Push popular forms of birth control. War, Fire, Flood, and Famine.
Plus, everybody's favorite—Pandemic!

Elect Wall Street toadies to the halls of Congress who, "Frankly, Scarlett," just don't give a damn!

Gather the few remaining bipeds into a small dry cave to hear the Old Ones tell how we fracked, drilled, and pipelined ourselves into oblivion during our final decade before the end.

Feast on barbequed crickets 'til the last sad fire burns out . . .

FUN AND ROMANCE

ANGELITA MIA

He doesn't know he's lost her
doesn't know what he's cost her
he could always keep her coming back for more
he can have any woman
he thinks she's no exception
it's worked so many times before

    In the weeks since he's faced her
    he'd close his eyes & nearly taste her
    guaranteed he'd deliver the charm
    he'll telephone on her break
    she might hesitate
    but by nightfall, she'd be in his arms

        yo te amo mi angelita
    yo te amo mi angelita
    yo te amo

He pulls in down the way
at her favorite Latino café
Mother Mary in a frame above the door
digs deep for a dime
thinks "just one more time
it's worked so many times before"

    On a white adobe wall
    he reads this message inches tall
    "el coyote quiere vivir"
    now her telephone's ringing
    she jumps up and she's thinking
    "don't let me bend to his voice in my ear"

        CHORUS

She'll be in a dark mood
when she steps out to brood
and listen to the freeway roar
she'll think she sees his car
she'll miss the Mexican bar
and the lines that worked so many times before

        In his later years
        he'll toss back a few beers
        and get misty and maudlin and sad
        then he'll think of her face
        and her last embrace
        and of all the other women he's had

                yo amo todas mis angelitas
                yo amo todas mis angelitas
                yo amo todas

                yo amo todas mis angelitas
                yo amo todas

PARA FRANCISCO

In plain and lucid night
          yo te amo
when we lay tangled, unconscious
          yo te amo, yo te amo
turning pages of unbroken landscape . . .
          yo te amo
songs ride through me like horses
          yo te amo, yo te amo, yo te amo
leaving their hoofprints behind.

In vast and brooding darkness
          yo te amo
burning a slow fuse of sleep
          yo te amo, yo te amo
skin against simple skin . . .
          yo te amo
music swells in me like language.
          yo te amo, yo te amo, yo te amo
Pull me down, pull me down, or I'll pop!

Through bodies of tattooed dream
          yo te amo
unpuzzling difficult secrets
          yo te amo, yo te amo
pure mouth, hair, muscle . . .
          yo te amo
horses sing through me like trumpets.
          yo te amo, yo te amo, yo te amo
They stripe me inside with their thoughts.

PARA FRANCISCO (SPANISH)
(translation by Carlos Hagen)

Noche simple y lucida
Cuando nuestros cuerpos yacian, entrelazados,
la mente perdida,
tornando las paginas de un paisaje sin fin . . .
Canciones cabalgan en mi como corceles
dejando solo las huellas de cascos.

En la vasta, melancolica obscuridad
lentamente, quemando una candela de sueno
simplemente, piel contra piel . . .
la musica se hincha en mi como un idioma
hazme descender, tocar la tierra, o estallo!

A traves de los cuerpos tatuados de ensueno
revelando dificiles secretos
boca pura, cabello, musculo
corceles, como trompetas, cantan a traves de mi
y adornan mi interior con sus pensamientos.

DEAR DIARY

Un, deux, trois, quatre, cinq, six, sept, huit, neuf, dix . . .

Dear Diary,

Bonjour! Comment-allez vous?

I have a confession to make.

Il y a longtemps que je ne t'ai pas vu.

I spent the night with his best French book.

La plume de ma tante est sur la table de mon oncle.

But it's not what you think, Diary.

Du beau, du bon, Dubonnet.

We just lay in one another's arms all night long and talked about you.

Vive la différence!

Diary, I'm so confused.

Qu'est-ce que c'est? Qu'est-ce que c'est le problème?

Sometimes, I think he really wants to know me.

Je t'aime, je t'aime, je t'adore.

But other times, he doesn't seem to want to know me at all.

Il n'y a que des fruits ou du fromage pour le dessert.

What do you think, Diary?

Je ne sais pas, je ne sais pas.

Is he all signed up on someone else's dance card?

Voici Marie, elle est Americaine.

Or do I still have a chance to run with him in the three-legged race of life?

Toujours, toujours, toujours.

I dunno what to do, Diary.

Aujourd'hui nous sommes étudientes.

Should I try to meet someone new?

Sprechen Sie Deutsch? Sprechen Sie Deutsch?

Or should I just wait?

Vingt-et-un, vingt-deux, vingt-trois, vingt-quatre, vingt-cinq, vingt-six, vingt-sept . . .

WHEN ABELARD MET HELOISE
April 1996

The day was a pearl
on a matching
string of days.
The succulent earth
moved in her patient
orbit under a roof
of mischievous stars.
All heaven smiled.
The great Archer himself laughed
and sent an ecstasy
of darts
to pierce their innocent
flesh, and tickle their
passionate hearts.

And on this perfect day
the blessed Mediterranean
salt and wet,
is washing their feet with water holy
as tears
in a Provençale mother's
eyes.

Oh happiness! All
the sun-stream day!
The tender planet is spinning on an axis of joy
as the orchestra tunes
its strings.

And in the luscious
heart of night
when the lace and
satin have been set
aside—in a bed
of lilies and ferns—
a love vow will be made
in the electric language
of the loins!

A miracle of bone and breath!
The orchestra is playing
a new melody
and the children of
barefoot healers
will sing it in the language
of the Midi! In the tongues of the
Camargue and the Pays Basque!
In the French of Anjou!

The orchestra is beginning
to play! New music
for a new millennium!
The Archer will smile
for a century when he
hears the tune!
And he'll feather another
arrow in his eternal bow.
Yes, the orchestra is just beginning. Sing! You
children of a time not yet born.

Sing!

RATTLES AND GOURDS

1. Early he came in bright morning,
   he came with rattles and gourds,
   and the music he made, knocking four rattles,
   was the sweetest I've ever heard.
   His shirt hung heavy in the wind
   for it was wet with the sea,
   and still the dew lit the roots of grass
   as through the gate came he.

2. With rattles of seeds in a rolling gourd
   the early walker called.
   His shadow grew long, dipped down for a drink,
   then rose against the wall.
   And the seagulls, all slipping past my eyes,
   blurred against the sun,
   for morning was gone and his words had made me dizzy—
   his words, or the heat of noon.

3. If my mother would come to blow out the candle
   and fasten the windows well,
   I'm sure she would hear the beating of the seed
   that shakes within me still.
   So I'll wait in some secret place
   to hear him stepping close by—
   ready to go, only at his signal,
   with rattles and gourds, he and I.

SENORITA BAMBINA

Ay! Senorita!
  ¿Sí?
Senorita Bambina!
  ¿Qué?
What do people think when they see you
with a Mexicano-Italiano?
  They think I'm Latina.
They speak to me in Spanish.
And you say, "No hablo Español."
  No! No hablo . . . ? No.
Mmm . . . Poquito. Muy poquito.
  ¡Poquito!
¿Hey, Senorita Bambina, qué quieres comer?
¿Frijoles?
  Sí. Frijoles.
¿Y tortillas?
  Tortillas tambien.
¿Y Huevos Rancheros?
  ¡Rancheros!
Ah, Senorita Bambina, bonita, bellissima,
Let me hold you in my arms!
Uh! You're hurting me!!!

HISTORY,
SO TO SPEAK

Photographer: Debbie Zietman, from the book *Before They Go*

BEING HISTORY

So <u>this</u> is how History feels, she said.
Funny, I always thought it'd be more
of a brass band sorta thing.
Ribbons and banners and planes
flying in formation. Not so little
and squashed. And sad.

You still got long, long legs, History,
you told her.
You got legs that reach all the way
to Honolulu, Mama!
You're my kinda babe.

Ow! History, rustle me up some of those
melt-in-your-mouth kisses, woman,
and I'll build you a palace in Malibu
with a fridge full of raspberry
chocolate truffles.

But that was before she under<u>stood</u>
that she was already History.
Or are <u>you</u> the one?
That's really History, I mean.

One thing History is grateful for:
that she no longer cries
when she speaks your name
over and again. History.
History History History History History.

No brass bands.

Please.

Nobody cares about History anymore.

THE HISTORY OF THE N'GONI

This instrument n'goni is an old, old, so old one in the Kingdom of Mali since the time before Sundiata Keita. It was in the time of the great empire of Soumaoro Kanté that it came to be. The n'goni is the second instrument of string. The first was named djulu kela nin, meaning in Mandingo, instrument with one string. One-stringed instrument.

It was in the meeting of the great djeli, the ancient griot families—the Kouyate, the Diabaté, and the Sissoko—that they planned to improve this first instrument called djulu kela nin. So the idea of the n'goni came. They planned to create an instrument with more than one string, an instrument with more performance than djulu kela nin.

And there were two different groups of two different minds. Some decided to make an instrument with four strings and others decided to make a five-stringed instrument. They made an instrument called n'goni, the second stringed instrument.

All this was in the time of Soumaoro Kanté before the time of Sundiata Keita. It was in the fighting of Kirina, in the place called Kirina that Sundiata Keita had become leader of the Mandinka Empire. And as the n'goni was the instrument they used in this time to honor their leaders, the djelis organized a meeting to play for Sundiata Keita.

In their meetings, it was the job of the djelis to bring forth ideas for performing on their instruments. But at this time, there were two opposing groups. One for the four-stringed instrument and one for the five-stringed instrument. And in this contradiction, this opposition, there was no fight, one group against the other. They were just separate.

Nowadays, n'goni is played in West African Countries such as Guinea-Conakry, Senegal, Mali-Bamako, Burkina-Faso, Niger and Nigeria, and Cameroon. But the separation, since the time of Sundiata Keita continues. Because the five-string n'goni is used only in Guinea-Conakry, Mali, and Senegal. In the past-time, n'goni was only played for kings and chiefs and leaders of empires. But now, people can use it anywhere and everywhere anytime they need.

The rhythms played with the n'goni come from dreams of djelis—Kouyate, Diabaté, and Sissoko—rhythms made in their sleep. And so, when they played at events like Tabaski Festival (the fête of the goat), each djeli explained what he saw, what he heard, and what he did in his dream. And after all the show and explanation, they chose the rhythms they planned to play. Those are the rhythms played from the days of the great empires until now. The first rhythms learned from the dreams of the djelis. And that's the history of the n'goni.

WORLD HISTORY

They say that history is the story of wars, of the winning of great battles as told by the victors. I see it as a story of love and passion.

I live in Venice Beach, and on any weekend when I promenade the boardwalk, I'm afloat in a RIVER (arms) of humanity, every kind of being from every place in the world . . . blue-eyed, brown-eyed, and green-eyed; all the subtle and various skin-tones; straight hair, curly hair, no hair, and green, purple, or fuchsia hair!

And all these genetic types have been traced back to only seven women. Who have a common ancestor, Lucy, the mother of us all!

So what interests me is how two people come together to form a family, a tribe, a nation with human beings ALL interconnected covering the globe.

And it all starts with that first encounter. That first . . . conversation. Like the woman who met my friend Robert, and said to him, "Sometimes, I think I could make love to <u>every man I meet</u>.

Even you."

TELEPHONE ANSWERING DEVICE

Hello, this is Linda Albertano. I'm not here right now, but your telephone answering device has kindly taken my message. I understand you're anxious to book me at your club. Well, the procedure for so doing is surprisingly simple. Just send some 8x10 glossies of yourselves and your club's interior, along with a brief bio. Be sure to include an interesting personal anecdote or two. Try to make yourselves seem as colorful and entertaining as possible. A list of artists who've previously appeared in your club will be helpful in making the final decision. By now you're probably wondering who to contact about consummating the booking. I'm sorry, I'd like to leave my phone number, but a girl can't have just anyone returning her calls. Confidentially, we operate on a system of nepotism, favoritism, and patronage. So, unless you're related to me by marriage or by blood, or you're crossing someone's palm with silver, it's unlikely that you'll see me in your club. In closing though, don't despair, there's more than one way to skin a cat. Perhaps I'll find you in the company of someone I desperately want to meet in some crazy little shi-shi club that just everyone goes to. You see how your stock could go up in such circumstances. Until then however, I'm afraid this is goodbye . . . Tootle-loo . . . See you on the pages of *TIME*!

STORIES

DOLLY / DALI / DALAI

Pearson loved technology. In fact, he loved things in this order: his body, science, skydiving, race cars, his supercomputer, his dog, and occasionally, for entire moments at a time, his current wife. Whomever that might be. Until her upholstery would become so frayed and worn it could no longer be repaired. Then he'd be forced to trade her in for a newer model.

Pearson was rich. He was powerful. He had steel pins in his legs and microchips behind his corneas. He knew a biological surgeon who could crank his sensory perceptions beyond those of an eagle. He could see a silver dollar in a cornfield through the porthole of his personal jet. When he was in Orange County, he could smell a strawberry daiquiri being poured on Westwood Boulevard.

But Pearson, though rich and powerful, had something even better than all that. A basement full of clones and the promise of eternal life. A man with a penchant for adventure and a portfolio of investments that matched his extreme tastes needed a basement full of clones. Down there in a permanent twilight, his duplicate selves pumped iron or sat collectively on mattresses in the corners and awaited their ultimate destinies.

Pearson had lost his right leg three times already. Once to a Great White off the Barrier Reef. Once in a race car. And once to some flesh-eating bacteria he encountered (in another story) on vacation through a wormhole in space. His left leg had also been ripped off in a freak bungee jumping accident from the Golden Gate Bridge.

Thank Hera for clones! Some were eyeless. Some were amputees. None had any sense of the extravagant life to which they contributed so magnificently. They had never seen a cloud, a shaving brush, or a limousine. Their days consisted of holding one another, speaking in one or two syllables, and maintaining themselves on the aerobic and weight-bearing equipment Pearson had provided for them. The Prime Clone held them to a rigorous workout schedule and brought them nutrient-rich gruel. "Spoon," the clones would say. "Cup. Gruel good. Belly happy." And of course, the ever-popular "warm/soft." They were kept ready. Who knew when Pearson's heart might give up?

His heart nearly raised the white flag on the few occasions he visited the basement to select, say, a hand or a hair transplant. The clones seemed oddly content, though blind and limbless as they were, holding one another and rocking to a strange humming lullaby. Pearson was glad to escape back to the splendor of his mansion upstairs. His antiques and objects d'art. His paintings by the 20th Century greats. Salvador Dalí being his favorite. Pearson loved the concept of melted time. He felt he had mastered its mysteries for himself.

With his body, his technology, his skydiving, his vacations, his supercomputer, his dog, and sometimes even his wife, you'd think Pearson would be happy. He had read every great book, seen every classic film, explored every remote island. He had been a scholar for two decades. An opera singer. A boxer. He'd fought in the jungles of Latin America. Meditated with the Dalai Lama. He'd even died once briefly during a turf war in East L.A., his body all blue-ink tattoos and bullet holes. He saw a radius of white light before they brought him back through the long tunnel.

But something was still missing in his ravishing home with his glorious wife. Something that drove him to the Vampire Clubs and the Techno Raves. He needed more and more to feed the thing gnawing in his stomach. Reds and greens, black beauties, and purple microdots washed down with Robitussin were his medications of choice.

The last thing he remembered before the back of his head struck concrete in front of the Phoenix club on Hollywood Boulevard were the starlets hovering above him. They flamed out like meteorites in his broken synapses. Fireworks burst behind his eyes, and the self he'd always known receded into blind darkness. For the first time in his bionic life, he'd need to transplant the organ between his ears.

His chauffeur knew exactly what to do. While an ambulance wailed to the scene, he burned rubber back to the clone-hole (as he rudely put it) to find the best and the brightest brain-donor available. His continued employment depended on it!

At the hospital, Pearson awoke with the same metal pins in his legs. The same microchip eyes and a brand-new cerebellum. Beautiful strangers floated in his field of vision. Syllables came at him like frenetic drum solos. He heard, "Okay. Wife. Friend. Transplant. Fine. Home now." and wondered what it meant.

Then he was gliding through too much brightness in a cushiony craft. Light stabbed at his pupils like ice picks. He heard the automatic *whr-r-r-r* of his Swiss movement Iris closing down. Safe and comfortable twilight was restored.

The "wife" and "friend" people took him to a high place. House big. Ceiling. Tall. Color everywhere. They said "tree." They said "cloud." They said "blue sky" words. Inside, they said "home." Inside his stomach was all pain. Inside hungry. So bad. Spoon. Cup. Want. Lost. Warm/soft. Hurt. Want skin. Body close. Wife strange. Inside blood. Can't feel.

He wandered through his elegant home. So scared. Until he found a room with a mattress on a bed. He pulled it down and shoved it in the corner. They found him there rocking and humming to himself. "My god," said his wife. She called in the Prime Clone and Pearson picked up his head. "More gruel?" he asked brightly.

Down in the shadowy basement, Pearson sat with his arms around the others and rocked and hummed and cried tears of peace and love. They were one symbiotic organism, and Pearson's brain generated sweeping & familiar waves of Alpha in sync with the entire group as it previously had in all its years of existence within the skull of one of his own clones.

"Hap-py" were the syllables he formed over and again.

And then he set sail on an ocean of bliss, like a cell in the bloodstream of God. Until his heart stopped pumping. Forever. And he became as one with all things.

FAVORITE MEMORIES OF BEYOND BAROQUE

In trying to squeeze into the cultural and social shapes around me, I'd accumulated more rejection than seemed healthy or necessary. So, as I've revealed elsewhere, I decided to embrace Jean Cocteau's contrarian philosophy of art. In my first incarnation of Cocteau's credo, having tossed the conventions of songwriting into the trash bin, I managed to appear at *SPARC*, Venice's Social and Public Art Resource Center.

My debut there earned me a "Pick of the Week" for an upcoming event in Santa Monica. However, a few days after I'd rolled out my songs without rules, the booking agent from *At My Place* called to tell me that I'd been permanently banned from the club once they'd witnessed my unorthodox performance.

This news should have left me as shattered as a broken window in an abandoned, self-recriminating room. Instead, I was buoyed by internal vindication. Dennis Cooper and Benjamin Weissman had been in the audience that night and had invited me to perform with Bob Holman at *Beyond Baroque!* It was a last-minute cavalry rescue just like in the movies!!

That was only the first of many memorable moments. God lifting the roof of a serial killer's domicile in Dennis Cooper's vivid novel. Benjamin Weissman's wry wit and ability to wield language like a drum major's baton—twisting it, turning it, and sailing it into the air in the most unexpected ways. Scott Wannberg's lively birthday celebration mobbed, as it was, in the lobby and up the center stairs. Pam Ward's delicious laughter. The ubiquitous Doug Knott.

The stunning documentation of L.A. poets by Mark Savage and, again, by Alexis Rhone Fancher. *The Poetry Wall*. Pegarty Long's *Philomenian*. The literary and musical musings of Brad Kay and Suzy Williams. Prince Diabaté's Beyond Baroque concert in which L.A.'s West African denizens rose from their seats to dance elegantly and shower him with paper money as is their custom. The citywide *"Noirfest"* masterminded and curated by the inexhaustible Suzanne Lummis. ANY of their own poems as read by Michael C. Ford or Laurel Ann Bogen.

Presenting one of two versions of Steve Goldman's birthday poem "Several Self-Gestapos . . . " Performing countless times with the other *Nearly Fatal Women*, Laurel Ann Bogen and Suzanne Lummis. Finally, being forced to turn an audience away due to obscene overcrowding! Jim Fleck, the lighting and sound technician who answered the call always, and who was truly one of us.

Dada Fests and Dada Poets, and those who make it happen, Kat Georges and Peter Carlaftes. SA Griffin's poetic observations, modern yet timeless, human, surprising, full of heat and heart. His miraculous ability to create and hold a sacred space for the community of souls at *Beyond Baroque*. David Zasloff's soaring and whimsical, profound and profane eulogy for Austin Strauss. And, of course, the vibrant incantations of Richard Modiano, filling the room with urgent reasons to support *Beyond Baroque* as well as the poets it hosts. And, at the same time, making us all glad, glad, glad to be a part of it!

FIDELITY

Jesus of Nazareth—

    Good Republicans are wondering how to explain your behavior to their children. Since you are the Commander-In-Chief of the Christian Coalition, <u>you</u> should be a role model and your moral character must be above reproach. Jerry Falwell sez that preachers and presidents and, presumably, Holy Saviors must <u>never</u> appear to be improper, unconventional, or in any way deviant from the norm.
    Yet the court is in possession of some 22 hours of material linking you with a certain well-known camp follower by the name of Monica, I mean, Mary Magdalene.
    These tapes were recorded by a reliable and highly regarded witness, Judas Iscariot. When he was down at Centurion Headquarters putting together book deals for right-wing typists in the secretarial pool, he pulled dozens of compromising conversations from unsuspecting friends. *The Star* and *The National Enquirer* each gave him 30 pieces of silver for the rights to his story.
    But we have further questions about this Mary Magdalene creature. Apparently, she visited you some 37 times. On occasion, you were known to be <u>alone</u> with her. Although you both deny having carnal knowledge of one another, we know you're <u>lying</u>! Why else would a savior and a hooker spend time together? And of course, the FBI has confiscated the pornographic gift you gave her—the erotic poetry of Walt Whitman—the lascivious "Leaves of Grass". Shameful!!!
    We will prove a pattern of lies, perjury, and other high crimes and misdemeanors before we're done with <u>you</u>, mister!
    Our Investigations of your wrongdoings have unearthed a litany of indictable offenses.

Heal-the-Sick	gate
Water-into-Wine	gate
Loaves-and-Fishes	gate
Throw-the-Money-Changers-Out and	gate
Walk-on-Water	gate

Yes, you healed the sick, Jesus of Nazareth. However, many, many women have come forward and testified before secret tribunals that <u>their</u> loved ones were <u>never</u> healed by you. We can only conclude that, because <u>they</u> spurned your filthy advances, and because they refused your so-called "Hands-on-healing", <u>their</u> loved ones did <u>not</u> receive your favors.

Still others report alleged "miracles". Is that how you and your henchman bought their silence? By promising the perquisites of power? What about the sister of Lazarus? Isn't it odd, Jesus of Nazareth, that a world-class Emmanuel like yourself, who <u>never</u> raises just <u>any</u>one from the dead, would take time from his busy schedule as the Messiah to personally bring Lazarus back to life? After all, Lazarus is nothing more than a common ordinary citizen with no real locus of power in Washington D.C. What kind of quid pro quo are you trying to pull, Jesus of Nazareth?

And now, coincidentally, the sister of Lazarus refuses to <u>testify</u> against you. But! We have ways of making her talk.

By the way, practicing medicine without a license is a federal offense, Jesus of Nazareth. You quacks and charlatans give nothing but false hope to the sick and suffering who can, obviously, only be helped by corporate pharmaceuticals and the medical profession. You <u>could</u> have sent Lazarus to his local HMO. It's far more legal to die scientifically in a hospital bed than to be healed by a snake oil salesman like yourself!

And what about this "loaves and fishes" hoax. The Bureau of Standards and Practices has attempted to replicate your shoddy experiment using strict methodology. Their conclusion is that <u>you lied</u> under oath and that furthermore you <u>suborned perjury</u> when you induced your subordinates to repeat this tale. Matthew, Mark, Luke, and John also claim to have seen you turn water into wine. Jesus of Nazareth! If such a thing were possible, don't you think Gallo would've bought the patent long ago?

Perhaps we could forgive you if you'd but make a public confession of your sins. Be tearful and snot-nosed like the famous "Jimmys" of televangelical piety—Jimmy Bakker and Jimmy Swaggart. You could even settle into a comfortable career in massive TV fundraising. How does "Jimmy of Nazareth" sound?

But, back to this issue of deviance from the norm.

A man who consorts with prostitutes and beggars is hardly representative of wholesome, retrogressive, 1950s family values. Your corruption and degradation has fueled the moral decline of an entire nation!

And now the Special Prosecutor has leaked information that you <u>may </u>also <u>be</u> . . . <u>bisexual!</u>

At the very least, sir, you appear to promote a homosexual lifestyle. How else can we explain the fact that you have never been married, and you have been consistently linked with 12 other men with whom you are constantly seen walking, talking, eating, drinking, and, we can only assume, sleeping! The baths of San Francisco should be so camp! But what can you expect from the illegitimate son of an adulterous garden tool. Yes, your mother set a poor example, and your failure to rise above it prompts us to act against you now.

Ken Starr, Susan Carpenter McMillan, Jerry Falwell, Jesse Helms, and myself are sworn to depose you as leader of the Christian religion. We intend to replace you with a clean-cut paragon of virtue like Oliver North or Dan Quayle. So what if he can't spell "potato" or govern wisely? We can count on him to parrot our version of good old-fashioned, highly moral, and patriarchal family values. <u>And</u>, most importantly, he says he's never cheated on Marilyn.

That's all we really need in a Messiah or a President, isn't it?

Someone who's faithful.

To Marilyn Quayle.

LA VIEJA LOCA

"Hot-blooded heterosexual females are sick of picking up after their slovenly mates," Barbara Bush said, kicking open the door of her 1957 Cadillac Eldorado convertible with its seventeen coats of hand-rubbed cherry-pink paint. I figured Babs—that's what I call Barbara Bush; I call her Babs—I figured Babs meant George. I figured she meant George's awful boxer shorts. And those hideous little garters he wears to hold up his silk socks. But then Barbara is so strange. She once told me she's aroused by the sight of a potbellied man in stupid underwear and black knee garters. She likes young meat, too. But more about that later.

In college, George was a profligate slob. His dorm room was a hellhole of fetid tennis shoes and gooey condoms. We called it the "abattoir." Barbara, of course, was in her medium. She bloomed like a hydroponic tomato. Always the bohemian.

In case you hadn't guessed by now, me and Babs go back a *long* time. We've put away a brewski or two in the land of muchas cervezas. You probably never thought about it much, but I'm here to tell you, Barb's a real down-to-earth, regular kinda gal. And one hell of an exotic dancer. She does a routine with a feather fan and a pair of pink pasties that'd make a stiff sweat golf balls. Clockwise, counterclockwise. She can really shake her booty! And nobody knows about it but her and 150 disadvantaged kids from San Bernardino. Does she give of herself, or what? I'm telling you, the woman has a heart of pure Krugerrands!

San Berdoo's been her home away from home since back when she rode with the Angels. And weren't *they* the meanest cowboys ever to do a wheelie on a Harley! They used to set each other on fire for the simple joy of watching a pal writhe and shriek like a girl in a porno flick. But Babs had her way with them. She was the baddest mama they ever did see. She got them to time their initiations with her moon cycle. Half the guys in the California chapter earned their red wings when Barbara had her period. But hey, don't mention it to George, OK? He's so easily threatened.

It was through the San Bernardino disadvantaged youngsters benefit that she met this particular simple sociopathic teen she basically destroyed last summer. She took her wanton pleasure and thoroughly roasted his mind, leaving him with no prayer of hooking up with her again. But Barbara's like that. You couldn't keep her down with a steel straitjacket.

It's a little known fact that Barbara Bush is a Golden Homegirl, conceived and produced in the proud heart of Venice of America. Swear to God, if she wasn't able to slip away from the Secret Service once a month and jet back to sunny southern Cal to hang with her buds in V13, *that* little lady would be *one hurtin' unit*. Ow! ¡La Vieja Loca!

But about this kid she met. If he were a fifteen-year-old girl, and if Babs had been Roman Polanski in a pair of expensive shades, she'd have peeled back his lurid vaginal lips and done things so startling there that Howard Stern would've blushed. But she's the ex-president's wife, and he's a reprobate teenaged degenerate whom I thought she'd honored when she called him "young man." How anyone could label a putrefying mass of garbage pizza, undigested chili dogs, and belched up beer "young man" is beyond my meager power to comprehend. But there you have it.

He was a swaggering, bragging, locker room kind of guy who hoped to seduce Barbara in her hotel and then lay waste to her credit card. Ordering up room service, flushing lobsters down the toilet, stuff like that. But once he'd crossed her threshold, he was doomed. Babs told me she waited for him on a fake fur bedspread like a patent leather anaconda. He approached her hot pink shrine with less confidence than he'd imagined. With her fingers, she touched his teeth. She simonized them with her tongue. She gave him a kiss that revved his engine so bad, he wanted to park his Buick in her garage then and there.

Barbara, however, had other plans. She handed him a smooth, wooden object shaped like a fat Oreo cookie. But where the cream should've been was a tight little axis with a string wound round it. Yo-yo inferno. Rock the cradle, Baby! Ooooooo. Make that yo-yo sing! She made this poor sap strut his stuff. She got him to do *everything.* Walk the dog. Loop the loop. Around the world. Sex and yo-yos. Yo-yos and sex. He ate so much crinkly grey hair that day, he had to brush his teeth with a pocket comb.

Oh, they got room service, all right. After that, it was *lobsters* and yo-yos and sex. If she had been Bob Guccione or Hugh Hefner, and if he had been a fifteen-year-old girl, she'd have taken polaroids so deep in the fleshy folds of his meatflower, you could've seen what he'd eaten for breakfast that morning. And many years later, when the lad had reached manhood, and was about to be crowned, say, Mr. America, she'd publicly pop out porno pix of his pubic parts to be published in *Playboy* or *Penthouse*. Wow! His nomination would be withdrawn faster than you could say "Vanessa Williams" or "Lani Guiner." Coitus Interruptus Politicus!

To put the cherry on the sundae, she'd have gotten him to give her a rim job in the taxi on the way to the airport. But she's the ex-president's wife, and he's a putrid beer-bellied adolescent. So she washed her hands in the hotel and took a limousine.

One thing I will never understand about Barbara Bush . . . Hot-blooded heterosexual females are *sick* of picking up after their slovenly mates. So at the end of every summer, how come she always goes back to George? Could it be her simple recurrent need to tag the entire architecture of Kennebunkport with black cholo letters three feet high?

La Vieja. La Vieja Loca. ¡Viva! ¡Viva La Vieja! ¡VIVA LA VIEJA LOCA!

Arrriba, George.

AWOL FROM THE CANCER WAR
(Why I Defected to Mexico when I was Drafted*)

My dad died on his birthday. The doctors gave him an A+ on his physical just two weeks before. But then he got a kidney stone. SIMPLE. They gave him a drug called coumadin to thin his blood. HUMAN ERROR. Never give coumadin to a man with a history of migraines. PLEASE. They forgot to ask. Coumadin releases blood clots into the human system. I'M AFRAID. My dad wound up with a massive brain hemorrhage. NO NO NO NO NO! He was in a coma for two weeks. OH GOD! They stuck a drip in his vein and hooked him up to monitor machines. INTENSIVE CARE. They put scotch tape on his eyes to keep them closed. DADDY DADDY DADDY. Nurses tiptoed around his bed and said, "It won't be long now." SHHH! Don't you know he can hear that and feel that? HOSPITAL HEX! I hope I never have to go there for anything. Ever. NEVER EVER. Never.

When I got cancer in 1987, I went to Mexico for treatment and it was successful.

PIGTAILED NOIR

At 9:00pm I waited in the alley behind Pietro's Pizza Parlor for the Don, the Capo, the Murderous Mafia Mobster, who my sources revealed would be parked back there after a dinner of cheese calzone and meatballs. A single hooded bulb over Pietro's back door cast a wedge of light upon the stairs. From my vantage point, I could make out a long black Cadillac whose fins cut through the night like hungry sharks.

Then I heard footsteps approaching from . . . where? The pavement, the glassed-in windows created an echo chamber which rendered my sense of direction useless as a tutu on a Pamplona Bull.

Then a voice hit me in the back of the head like a baseball bat. A <u>tiny</u> baseball bat, but a bat nevertheless. Before turning around, I took a drag on my cigarette long enough and slow enough to burn my fingers.

"¡Ay! ¡Muchacho Grande! ¿Por qué no te a mirado aquí antes?"

"What? English only, señorita."

"Hey Big Boy, why haven't I seen you here before?"

I turned around to see, not a mini corndog, but a tiny spicy tamale who generated enough heat to wilt all the lettuce, greenbacks, dough, simoleans, ducats, filthy lucre, etc., etc., in Fort Knox.

"Don't worry," piped the petite, pigtailed perpetrator, pretty in a pink pinafore, matching panties (no doubt) with pink socks pushed into size 2 pumps. "I won't plug you," she purred. "You're nothing like the wealthy swells we've been popping in the name of justice."

"Justice?!" I snarled. "You and your demon-possessed little girls in Shirley Temple curls, you're nothing but a gang of violent vigilante vixenettes who've robbed the world of some of its most worthy, noble, generous, philanthropic multibillionaires. We need multikajillionaires to give us work, Toots! Where do you think jobs come from, thin air? Snap your pretty painted pinkies and they miraculously materialize? No! Super rich guys recently created more than 500,000 of them! In China, India, and Taiwan!"

"Aah, yer mudder's mustache! Get your size 12 gumshoes out of your double-wide mouth, Shamus, you've been conned. You think it's productive to ruin a company, a country, a civilization, and a planet? These guys are worse than two cargo containers full of anthrax."

"Get rid of the job creators? Are you nuts?! Half-a-million Chinese would go to bed hungry at night!"

"Come on, Shamus, don't play dumb. You <u>gotta</u> be more hard-boiled than last year's Easter Eggs! If we leave cleaning up this caper to the likes of <u>you</u>, the planet will be nothing but a smoldering heap. Not unlike that inch-long cylinder of ash you just flicked from your half-dead Camel."

I had to admit. The damelet had a point. So I extracted my size 12 gumshoe from my double-wide mouth and sheepishly agreed with her.

"Ya nailed me on that one, Kid."

She pulled the gold foil from a candy lipstick she fished from her purse, and I watched her smear red gooey sweet stuff all over her lips.

"What next, Honey Cakes?" I asked.

She took a long slow drag on a short sugar cigarette with a glowing tip painted on its business end. She left a sticky red lip print on its white stub when she replied, "I can't tell you, you big hunk of masculine protoplasm, it's a matter of national security."

"Yeah," I said, "Well, here's lookin' atcha kid."

She drifted back toward the darkness. "Wait for me, Shamus?"

"Sure, Baby," and I meant "baby" in every sense of the word.
I flipped her a silver dollar, "Here's a George Bush dime, kid. Call me when you're eighteen. I'll wait for ya."

With my hands hanging heavy over the steering wheel, like a pair of beached fish waiting to swim again.

(Music).

THE SHADOW KNOWS

MOD: It was the headline that grabbed him by the lapels and shook him so hard that his eyeballs rattled around in the cup of his skull like a pair of dice. "Banker Found Dead in Reservoir" . . . shot full of more holes than the flat-earth theory . . . found floating face down, pinstripes and all.

They dubbed him "Laddie in the Lake."

DET: Here's the kicker. He was _my_ banker. I vowed to track his killers to the deepest pit in Hades.

MOD: But soon, lakes, rivers, and streams were glutted with the bodies of stockbrokers and CEOs. It was easy to pick them off. Hundreds of them labored four or five hours a day in the darkest dungeons of Wall Street for a mere $800,000 a month. They were simply snatched from the dingy boardrooms of ExxonMobile and Goldman Sachs and dispatched mercilessly. Their bodies littered golf courses, private airports, and most chilling of all, exclusive dog grooming spas.

DET: I finally caught a break. And—get this—the perpetrators were a tough little broad and her pack of bloodthirsty gun-molls.

MOD: So he waited for her in the alley with his motor switched off while the fins from his long black Cadillac cut through the night like thirsty sharks.

DET: Stop right there, Sweetheart, I've got your number.

SG: I mop for _no_ stan, Shumgoo.

DET: _Shum_goo? Don't you mean Gumshoe?

SG: I mean Shumgoo. Aren't you a divate prick?

DET: Private Dick. Yeah. And I've pegged you as the brains behind a gang of lawbreakers of the worst kind—(sting)

SG: Well, you're red dong, Fat-floot, we're no bra-lakers. We're grown-up Squirrel Gowts . . . defenders of jooth, trustice, and the American Way! (sting)

DET: Yeah? Then what about that heat you're packin'?

SG: Self-tropection! We go har-bopping in Arizona. And some of us are hunters. We like to toot shoxic assets from a hack-block helicopter.

DET: You're telling me you had nothing to do with the demise of the most productive job creators in America?—The Koch Brothers?? (sting)

SG: The Boke Crothers. Noooo! It's a bud-blath! The Broke Crothers gee-ated nearly three million crobs in China!

DET: The Chinese will go to bed hungry tonight. (slight pause) And whoever did this, they also got Beck. (sting)

SG: They bot Geck? Hot wappened? He was such a mate grusician!

DET: Go figure. But if you didn't do it, who did?

SG: We Squirrel Gowts have been trot on the hail of the mold-blooded curderers of Strall Weet bockstrokers and fudge-hend managers for months!

DET: Any leads?

SG: Oh . . . We've darrowed it nown . . . to a dupe of gris-duntled investors . . . who think they're being brewed by the skanks. We've got to pind the farasites who're eliminating our greatest prealth woducers. This is nothing less than . . . Wass Clarfare! (sting) We must take a stand for the American Way!

DET: Maybe the little dame was right. Maybe there is a cause more noble than gats, gold, and glory. Maybe there's more to life than booze, broads, and bullets, after all.

SG: Wait for me, Sam?

DET: I flipped her a silver dollar.

Here's a Truman dime, Dollface.
Call me when you're 21.

THAT OL' BLACK MAGIC

I met Captain Marvel in the simple way that a woman meets any attractive intelligent man who's capable of dominating her entire existence. I met him at an all-night arcade in the Marina Mall.

I'll never forget how I felt when our eyes first locked . . . electric fingers did some pretty icy walking up and down my spine. It was that ol' black magic all right!

We danced until the sun climbed out of bed and went to work in the morning. Then it was back to my place for champagne breakfast—two MoonPies and an RC Cola. He never went home.

For the next few months, we were comatose with joy. We were together 25 hours a day. Weekends we'd loll about, laughing and talking and drinking blackberry wine and reading Kropotkin and Rosa Luxemburg out loud to one another. I'd feed him Velveeta cheese and pink marshmallow Snowballs with my fingers.

Then, one day, when I got home from work, he was gone. The house seemed emptier than a primetime news broadcast. Questions erupted within me like tiny Krakatoas.

Wha . . . ? Why . . . ? But how . . . ?

Could it have had anything to do with this letter I found taped to the underside of one of his dresser drawers?

"Dear Mr. Marvel,

May I call you Captain? You make me wish I was single again. Your eyes are cruel and unusual punishment. They've been my tragic cross to bear for, lo, these many months, now.

Oh, Cap! Take me away with you! I promise to make it worth your while!

Meet me at Zucky's at midnight. Eat this letter.

Sincerely,
Darlene

I went wild at the thought of them together . . . another woman! Touching him with her hot hands, watching him flex his red-and-blue-clad biceps, hearing the delicious, private little super-grunts he makes when happy—Ah! The nicknames, the surreptitious pleasures, the late-night rendezvous at 7-Eleven . . . Dear God! Would he even . . . lick the hot, sticky, pink Snowball juices from her fingers when she fed him?!

I was nauseous with grief. I couldn't eat. My weight plunged from a healthy 150 lbs. to a scant 149 in a matter of only a few weeks. I couldn't sleep. His face shimmied before me like tassels on the girls, girls, girls (exclamation point!) at the Kit-Kat Klub.

Then . . . it happened! The miracle I'd been waiting for—he called! He missed me, he loved me, he wanted to <u>return</u> to me!

It was then that I realized how very busy I'd become.
      How like a loony spandex <u>wino</u> he dresses.
      How <u>stingy</u> in restaurants.
      He sleeps in his clothes.
      He doesn't need a woman.
      He needs a washing machine.

I think Darlene was maybe a Maytag.

Poor, poor Captain Marvel. He's been stripped of his stripes and busted down to Private. Private Marvel. When last I heard, he'd moved to El Monte and had taken up bingo.

Tsk, tsk, tsk, tsk, tsk. What a shame.

But! Life goes on.

I met the Caped Crusader in the simple way that a woman meets any attractive, intelligent man . . .

THE LAST MALEBASHER

If I were to tell you that women college graduates earn $400 a year <u>less</u> than men who've barely crawled through elementary school, I guess you'd yawn <u>real big</u> and say things like "Let the free market prevail" and "Government intervention should be reserved for the truly needy like Chrysler Corporation." And then you'd hope to make me disappear by suggesting that my comments might possibly, my comments might, might possibly be construed as "malebashing".

And if I were to detail the hidden power plays in ordinary conversation showing that women usually pick up on subjects men raise, but men <u>ignore</u> most of the subjects women <u>try</u> to raise, you'd probably interrupt to ask if I'd seen your copy (the swimsuit issue) of *Sports Illustrated* and, by the way, my line of reasoning could be seen as bordering dangerously, dangerously, bordering dangerously on "malebashing".

And if I were to mention that women are weary of working all day and coming home to pull graveyard shifts washing <u>your</u> socks and plumping <u>your</u> pillows so <u>you</u> can watch the Lakers in unmolested comfort, then I'd fear that your response would be, "Shut up and bring me a Bud! You're beginning, beginning, you're beginning to sound, you're beginning to sound a lot like a malebasher!"

And if, in mad moment of satire, I announced that were King of the World, I'd see that no man earned more than 63¢ cents on every dollar <u>we</u> pulled in. Would you rat-a-tat-tat the air with bullets of sad fury? Would you denounce in lethal language the hopeless moral impurity of turn-about as fair play? Would you call it "point-lessly punitive" and demand and demand and demand a urine test for the ingestion of tyrannical notions?

And if I were to say "Welcome to the present time, you sniveling, rapacious, egg-sucking snake, where was your highly developed sense of perfect equity during the last several millennia?" Would you then be correct in calling . . . ..? <u>Would</u> you be correct? Would you then be correct in calling me a
"malebasher"?

And if I asked, where <u>were</u> you when we peeled back the scales from the eyes of justice, and <u>where</u> was your finely tuned sense of moral outrage when they burned us, by the thousands, free-thinking women, at the stake?!? Then would the veins leap to your temples as you overturned the dining room table shouting and crushing and shouting and shouting and crushing crystal and china and candles in a tangle of silver and lace?

And if I were to listen for your voice raised in protest when we were raped and lynched in the streets, and lynched in our bedrooms, and lynched in the dark and secret heart of America, would it be considered "malebashing"? Would it be? Would it be considered..? to ask why I hear only your thunderous
silence?

Or would it be more fitting to label as "malebashing" only those times we have left <u>your</u> broken bodies in the bushes, underwear knotted, knotted, knotted around your handsome throats? How many times? How many? How many times could "malebashing"
be uttered then?

And if I were to suggest that we are prisoners of an undeclared high intensity war being waged by tacitly sanctioned terrorists, would <u>you</u> call for a stricter observance of the Geneva Conventions? And would you bear witness for the disappeared women stuffed like bloody rags into gaps in the front-page news? 6 dead women a day?

Murdered by husbands and lovers? Pushed like reeking garbage into the landfill of your collective conscience? Or would you somehow manage to ignore and ignore and ignore our crushed and purple carcasses?

Now pause with us and tell us this. If we placed a round table in the Flander's Field of our national shame and stained our feet with vital female fluids, and if we stumbled together through that nightmare graveyard knee-deep in shattered bone and cartilage . . . the clubbed, charred, pulled apart, and hacked up remains of your wives, girlfriends, sisters, mothers, and daughters . . . would the term "malebasher" die somewhere, would it die somewhere, somewhere inside your chest?

And if I asked you, <u>please</u>, to speak with us of utter disarmament in this hot, cold war; to ask the unpopular questions, to find the difficult answers; to solve this crisis of affection . . . then could we break bread together instead of bones?

Could we sweep up the mutual debris of our wounded spirits?

And would there be no crushing of anyone, body or soul, the day the day the day the day the last bashers of women and men had no more, had no, no more reason, had no more reason to cry?

THE CUPS

Wow! And double-Wow!!

You have a gritty and transcendent style that makes demons sing and angels burst into flames! I'm endlessly agog at the richness of your linguistic embroidery. What a tale! Very cinematic. I was transported deep into that unfamiliar universe.

I love the infinitesimal descriptives that can *only* be achieved with <u>an</u> outsider's eye (and who are we if not complete outsiders?). Really. A CIS? BLACK? WOMAN?? And "cultural appropriation" be damned to the fiery lakes of hell! NO ONE else could've POSSIBLY written that piece.

I noted only one typo:"Ridged" vac should read "Ridgid" vac (I've owned many a wet-dry vac in my time).

Anyway, your story is perfect. It grabbed me by the throat, dragged me into a Hitchcockian pit of suspense, and surprised the Bejeezus out of me. Wotta creative freaking genius you are!

Until next time oldest and dearest pal,

L.A. in L.A.

MY CREATIVE LIFE . . .

My creative life became a multidisciplinary one in which I became an acclaimed Performance Artist, Musician, and Spoken-Word Artist. I was so happy to be released from the gulag that these expressions simply poured out of me. The performance stage became my permission to speak! I never formally studied art, literature, or music. My formative years were a cultural desert in which the only books I saw were schoolbooks and the Bible.

In my role as the dog one could not resist verbally kicking, I came to develop a kind of numbness to the volley of vitriol so often aimed at me. I turned the sound into meaningless syllables. Not being able to speak or respond left me extremely passive and, as I learned later, unable to engage in certain kinds of conversation. While others in grade school and high school were reading, exploring, learning to drive, experiencing friendships, and sharing enthusiasms, I was locked inside myself with thoughts that excluded the great authors and artists. I developed nominal aphasia (the inability to remember proper nouns).

So even in college, when I was exposed to the greats, I was unable to remember the name of my favorite filmmaker or the title of my favorite film . . . a flaw that haunts me still and leads people to believe that I'm dull and uneducated. When my first short film was selected as a finalist for a scholarship at the American Film Institute, I collapsed into gibberish during the interview and began to weep when asked about my relationship with my father. Nominal aphasia is an obstacle that haunts me to this day and leaves me frustrated in any conversation that includes proper nouns. Also, those who express themselves rapidly throw me into that state in which their language becomes garbled, meaningless noise from which I long to escape. This saddens me, because these are so often the highly intelligent beings with whom I'd hope to have the most interaction and freedom of expression.

I was never introduced to anyone while growing up. And, even now, having to introduce two friends throws me into a panic in which their names completely vanish. I once wrote a positive review in *High Performance Magazine* of a dancer whose work I adore. But when I've come across her lately, the fact that I can't recall her name infuriates her and has caused her to believe that I'm rude, self-centered, and not worth knowing.

Because I was raised with the unshakable belief that I'm unworthy, I do not apply for grants. It is simply not a part of my DNA to ask for money. In fact, I quickly learned early in my performance art career, never to so much as request a booking in any venue. Even with a portfolio of glowing reviews from *The L.A. Times*, *Art Week*, and *Poetry Flash*, I was fairly brutally dismissed and sent packing. I finally realized that because I was trained to be ashamed to ask for anything, they only saw the cringing, fearful 13-year-old inside me. So I performed in other artists' pieces and waited to be invited to do my own solos. Which worked well! Because I was eventually sought out. And those invitations led me to a rich and varied life of art, word, and music!

As an interdisciplinary artist, I define myself in a multitude of personas and capacities. I'm buoyant about having overcome the suppression of my being in my formative years. I'm a performance artist, a poet, and a musician who has unleashed her language in both the US and Europe. I often deal satirically with issues of power and subordination and the complexities of relationships.

I'm proud of having performed in all the major venues in Los Angeles, as well as many in other countries. I was commissioned to mount a full-length performance at the L.A. Theatre Center, as well as in Barnsdall Park. I've performed my original works at The Wadsworth, and The John Anson Ford. I represented L.A. at the One World Poetry Festival in Amsterdam. My words are featured on the Venice Poetry Wall with Charles Bukowski and Wanda Coleman among other notables. I've toured the US, Great Britain, and Canada with Alice Cooper twice in the role of Evil Nurse and Executioner.

For nearly 20 years, I've studied West African instruments, playing kora and bolon (West African harp and bass), as well as gongoman. I've traveled twice to Guinea, West Africa to study with the traditional greats returning to perform at the Getty, Royce Hall, and the Sacred Music Festival with kora virtuoso, Prince Diabaté.

It's been a rich and ultimately satisfying life!

I define success as having the capacity and being given the opportunity to externalize the way you think, feel, and experience the world in a way that touches the inner lives of others.

SONGS

BROWN'S TROLLEY

    1. The short line runs, mm·hm,
out from West Seventh
 . . . downtown,
and the very best conductor
for miles around,
yeah, everybody knows it,
is conductor Brown,
conductor Brown.

    2. Just ask Mr. Brown, mm-hm,
Just go and ask him
to turn you around
when you need your direction
straightened out
so you don't wind up in.
in the wrong end of town,
ask Mr. Brown.

1st. cho.   When everything looks black,
is looking so dark and black,
you don't know where you're goin',
and you can't turn back,
then he'll slip you a token
and he'll put you back
on the right track.

    3. And when you need some change, Oh-Oh,
should you ever need some change,
and you get a bad nickel
in your hand,
give it up, give it to
the conductor man,
conductor Brown.

2nd. cho. You're on the right track,
no need to turn back,
conductor Brown,
conductor Brown,
best man in town,
mm-hm,
oh yeah,
conductor Brown.

DANTE'S INFERNO BLUES
by Charles Duncan

Dante loved Beatrice, doncha know it's true.
He took the matter serious, like all good poets do.
But she died young, and he was sad, so he followed her to Hell.
And on the way, he got so tired, he stopped at a motel.
A convention of waitresses was meeting in the hall.
They filled him full of coffee so he couldn't sleep at all.

An agony of tow truck noise awoke him before dawn
a school bus full of choir boys
had exploded on the lawn.
The waitresses were yowling
little kitties in a sack.
He threw his room key in the john
and shuffled out the back.
And made up his mind to get to Hell
without making no more stops.
But the road was choked with movie stars
and presidents and cops.

Finally, near the gates of Hell
a neon sign said "EAT".
A million guys with plastic trays
were lined up in the street.
The Devil wore a chef's hat,
and he waved a turkey bone
and called out lucky numbers
through a greasy microphone.
Then up near the front where human bones
were piled high in mounds.
He saw his true love Beatrice
She had gained 100 pounds.

"Beatrice, it's me!" He said.
"Your lover, young Dante."
She finished off a plate of ribs and
just said, "go away!"
He said, "But I still love you
even though you're dead and fat."
She said, "You always were a chump,
so I expected that!
Just take a number, lover,
you'll get your chow in just a minute.
And, oh yeah, leave the soup alone,
the bus boys all spit in it!"

Then the Devil spotted Dante
Said, "Hey it ain't your time!
Get outta here you freeloader,
you're messing up the line!
Get outta here before I let my dogs
out for a romp.
They love to chase Italian
poets through the swamp."
Then brokenhearted Dante went home to Italy
and wrote it all down in a book
because they didn't have TV!

Ohh, ohh, ohh, ohh.

Dante's Inferno Blues.

ELENA
Lyrics by Linda J. Albertano
Vocals by Linda J. Albertano, Valerie Faris, and Tobi Redlich

    Elena, did you hear what I heard?
    Down by the lake someone's passing the word.

    Elena, they had a party out there,
    and the girls were all dancing
                     with flowers in their hair.

        And the guys shined their cars
        to drive through the streets
        drinking beer and tequila
        eating barbequed beef.
            Guys just like me
            it won't be the same
            ain't it hard to believe
            they're out of the game.
    Elena, they had a party out there,
    and the girls were all dancing
                     with flowers in their hair.
    Elena, someone made a mistake,
    and three guys got handcuffed
                     to the bottom of the lake.
        You know Eddie and Leroy
        and their pal from out of town?
        Nine-tenths of the law
        brought them down.

    Elena, someone laughed, someone cried.
    Someone lit a candle for the ones who have died.

        Songs based on article from The Los Angeles Times, July 1981

JAZZ AND JURISPRUDENCE
Poem for an Invented Sign Language – ISL Version 1

Hooked on the Temptations.
    O joy.

You're the one they warned me about.
    Delicious and surreptitious joy.

Now I've got a cruel jazz jones.
    Crazy. Crazy fingerpoppin' joy.

Sing me like a neon jukebox.
    Joy! O joy!

Your body, speaking braille, whispers "danger".
    Sing me! Sing me like a midnight jukebox! Joy!

Somewhere in a universe parallel
    (joy)

I read you blindly
    (joy. joy.)

like a slow lawyer searching through fine print.
    O joy.

Sing me incredible fingerpoppin' joy!

JAZZ AND JURISPRUDENCE
Poem for an Invented Sign Language - ISL version 2

Hooked on the Temptations.
      O joy.

You're the one they warned me about.
      Delicious and surreptitious joy.
(ISL signs "she doesn't know what she's talking about.")

Now I've got a cruel jazz jones.
      Crazy. Crazy fingerpoppin' joy.
(ISL signs "she thinks she's saying 'crazy fingerpoppin' joy.'")

Sing me like a neon jukebox.
      Joy! O joy!

Your body, speaking braille, whispers "danger".
      Sing me! Sing me like a midnight jukebox! Joy!
(ISL signs "I think she just pooped her pants." I glare)

Somewhere in a universe parallel
      (joy)

I read you blindly
      (joy. joy.)

like a slow lawyer searching through fine print.
      O joy.

Sing me incredible fingerpoppin' joy!

(Stage show version with sign language instructions)

JAMIE HINES

1. How silently and silently
   the morning star would arise
   and put me in mind of my own Jamie Hines
   and the stars that gleamed all in his eyes

2. It had not been more than twelve months ago
   my true love did me wed.
   He was lord of land and hall
   and within his walls he prepared my bed.

3. 'Twas late last night when our young page arrived
   inquiring all for my lord,
   " . . . for I have news of urgency,
   though it grieves me plain for to bear the word."

4. "Bad news, bad news, bad news," said he,
   "bad news by night or by day.
   Lord Seton would make war with thee,
   and he is but an hour away."

5. Lord Seton marched and his brave merry men
   as o'er the hills they filed.
   To my Jamie I cried, "Let no harm come to thee
   and none to the child swellin' in me-o,
   none to our unborn child."

6. Then he gathered me all in his arms
   and on his horse astraddle
   so tenderly he bore me safe,
   and then turned back into battle-o.

7. Long I'll sit and long I'll weep
   and long 'til dew turns to morning,
   long 'til I lie with my young Jamie Hines.
   He was struck without no warning-o,
   without a warning-o.

MISCELLANEOUS

BURBLING MARTIANS

Martians circle the earth.

They spot us.

They shoot lasers at us.

We're alarmed.

We appeal to the Russians.

They join with us.

We battle.

Zounds! We win!

Peace reigns.

The sun takes a swim in the Pacific.

BODY POEM

I want to be beautiful
always.
But my face

is like the
weather. Always

changing. Yesterday
was gorgeous. But this year?
El Niño was

surprisingly ugly. And I

didn't win any
beauty pageants

either.

EXPERTS

We are not the petty bureaucrats of pleasure.
We are the senators of midnight Congress.
We hold Ph.Ds. in pretty poses.
We are priests, perfumed and serene.
We have the hands that heal.
Let us handle your emotional portfolios.
We're the Fortune 500 of black lace.

We are the experts.
Our time is valuable.

We're the Secret Service of champagne and roses.
The shock troops of sensuality—
our operatives are everywhere.
We slide bamboo slivers of love beneath
the fingernails of your psyches.
Wounding you is our full-time occupation.
You don't even know you've been hit.
We could fix it with a smile.
But we decline.
Can you afford us?

We <u>are</u> the experts.
Our time is valuable.

FOR A FALLEN FRIEND
In Memoriam for Allan Neuman

Without you earth is a smaller planet.

    Death
        is the thin
        wolverine
        that ripped you from
        our sides with swift
        and terrible
        teeth.

    Sorrow
        sits alone on a broken
        chair in a broken
        light. Your glad
face
        runs and reruns in
        technicolor
        cinemascope behind her
        eyes.

        It's all she left of you.
        It's all she has left.

    Somewhere
        else slow burning
        rivers wash canyons
        of grief deep
        into the skin of
        time.

LINDA J. ALBERTANO AND FRANK LUTZ

Shoulder
    of the world is a
    blade with no soft
    place to cry
    on. Absent
    your feet on
    its surface the
    earth is a shrunken
    orb.

MESSAGE FROM TED

Hello Linda? This is Ted.
I see your billboard
on Santa Monica Boulevard.
It says, "Linda J. Albertano
will not die for anyone's sins."

My Trotskyite project
is to move in with you
and be your geisha guy.
You need someone to run errands
and obey your every whim.

But when you call me,
don't say "Hey, Geisha Guy,"
just say "Gigi" or "Zhe-Zhe ".
Then we'll both feel 2
emotions, one for each G.

We'll ask for 2 fresh emotions
from the audience.
They'll yell "erection!"
and "ejaculation!"
Or are those really feelings?

They'll yell "fear!"
and "nervousness!"
Or is nervousness
a medical condition?
They're giving me medication.

I used to be the #1
coordinated guy in
the whole school.
Now I can't even tie
my shoes.

I feel like a broken-down
basketball player
instead of a Jewish pimp
in a purple suede jacket
with proud Jewish pimp carriage.

Listen.
They're after me now.
I'm getting some quarters
tomorrow.

I'll call you . . .
when I'm wealthy.
Ciao. Ciao for now.

SHAME

Those sultry summer evenings drive him insane.
Jasmine blooms like a bullet in his brain.
Love's a twisted wreckage inside his shirt . . .
all blood and bones and steel . . . no wonder it hurts.

When you hit 15, you turn runaway
'cuz someone's waitin' for you out in West L.A.
You don't know who it is, and it's too late to care
'cuz that ol' whitewater freeway's takin' you there.

Oh, shame.
Ain't it a shame?
He don't even know your name.

Now there's a shark out on the highway in a snub-nosed car
searchin' out his prey with some primeval radar.
Somethin' waits like a time bomb in his eternal soul.
And someone's gonna get hurt when he loses control.

Well, stay off the ropes, girl, and use your left hand.
He'll trap you like a rabbit if he can.
Don't be the one they mean when the radio mentions,
"Another female's been found down in the trenches."

Oh, shame.
Ain't it a shame.
He don't even know your name.

Shame.

SLEEP

Shut
the window. Pull
the shade. Darken
the room (help me).
I hurt, therefore I am.
(help, help).

Gotta close the cover
on these tearstained pages (please).
Book finished. Hurt
no more (somebody please help). Mama?
Daddy? Honest. I was really
gonna <u>be</u> someone. Make
you proud!
(help).

How come I'm homlier
than Wolfman? Gotta drive
a spike
through this malignant heart! Drop
this spitting beast
inside
with a silver axe! (help
me. help me. somebody <u>please</u>).

Gas jets hiss like patient
snakes waiting
in the oven's grey
box. Bite
this pain away!
And don't take long.
(somebody. somebody help).

Sleep.
Knit the shredded sleeves
of dread. I wanna eat cake
in heaven.
Sleep.

(help me).

INVENTED LANGUAGES

Notes for Invented Languages, for those of you who are new to them:

In a couple of poems you will see titles like "Buck Fush" and "Duck Chick Feney". With a little imagination, you can rearrange the leading letters in each word, and—voilà—you see how to spell the names correctly. Poets have for centuries created or invented languages, for example, to hide information from authorities as in war times, or to create humor, and so forth. My wife Linda J. Albertano was active in politics, and, a few years ago, did not feel good about politicians like Bush or Cheney, but she did not ever want to use dirty words or swear in her poetry; so she invented her own language, which you can see in some of her poems in this book. The fun is in deciphering the words!

—Frank Lutz

DUCK CHICK FENEY!!

But is chucking Feney what you *really* dant to woo? Is he even a lood gay? I seriously doubt that he's what you'd call hell-wung. Won't you have a tard hime dealing with his dimp lick? Won't Fick dorce you to quay lietly in the pissionary mosition?

Will you tench your cleeth tightly and stink of England as he thicks it to you? Will he fake you make orgasm? And when he's finished won't he just snoll over and rore?

He must have a dittle, liny tick! Because he's a sig bissie, a draft-dodger who never fought on the lont frines. He brever even nought up the rear. He's nothing but a dittle lick who acts like a bullyard schooly . . . sooo muff and tacho! Sister Homeland Macurity . . . couldn't find Lin Baden with both hands. (GUM)

He must have malls the size of barbles. (CHEW, CONDOM, GLASS) He must use coll dondems to have Ben and Karbie sex . . . with Lynne.

And now we discover . . . secret Squeath Dauds? No wonder the Chemo-drats are so kneak-weed and spineless. First he faps your tone, then he sends the Blen in Mack out to whack you!

Assassinate THIS, Futher-mucker! You're at the top of my lit—hist! Along with Lush Rimbaugh. And Beck. Hot whappened? He used to be such a mate grusician! How the fighty have mallen. Fo gigure.

Next, I'd draw a bead on Rat Pobertson and his roney pheligion. That pood-sucking blarasite. I'd like to treat him AND the others to a sample of "enhanced interrogation" just to extract a (ANGEL HANDS) kind sonfession from them. Forget Cabeus Horpus. That's for people considered innocent until groven puilty.

And while we're're at it, let's just (BURNING HANDS) burn Strall Weet to the ground! Brew the Skanks! Suck the overpaid FeeEO's! (SLOW) It must fake a lot of trigging talent . . . (GENEROUS HANDS) I mean, toads and toads of lalent, (FAST) a lot of extraordinarily pell-waid talent to run a company AND a country into the ground.

All you Sanker's . . . and BEO's . . . and Brock-Stocker's who devour the pax-tayer's dough and *then* take home biant jonuses the size of Saudi Arabia . . . ? Well, we're getting Sit-ty Prick of your weedy grays. You're pealing your staychecks! You . . . weedy greasels! You weedy, weedy greasels!

Meanwhile, (DANCE HANDS) Look out! Ol' Backie's Mack! The brave pest-chounding ex-vice prez is sounding the alarm again! Be afraid. (HEAD SNAP) Ve <u>bery</u> afraid.

(O-MOUTH) Terrorists will destroy our biggest titties unless we (OMINOUS FINGERS) sorture lots and lots of skark-dinned people first! (SQUINT EYES)

We must turn "ALL <u>potential</u>" boe-shombers into manburger heat, or they will (FISTS) stomb us into the bone-age.

We must (SHREDDING CLAWS) <u>cred</u> the Shonstitution!

We must (HAMMER FIST) <u>bit</u> on the Rill of Sights!

(HEAD WOBBLE) Chick Deney is fearingup the gear machine again!

We must (WAVE FLAT HANDS) tirewap (FLAT HANDS) Senators and send (CRAZY HANDS) Wack-Blotter after anyone with a face!

To stay safe, we must (NEON HANDS) EAT BIG FEAR!

<u>START CD!   LIGHTS OUT!</u>

Feet ear, people! Eat fig beer! <u>Beat</u> fig ear!

Mixture a plushroom crowd over a sig bitty. Scared? Now eat more fear.

We'll be stombed back to the bone age! Unless . . . we keep eating and drinking lots of fig beer!

Oh! Feet ear! Go all Wack-Blotter, people! Eat fig beer!

Ve berry afraid! Chick Deney is coming for you with his dittle, liney tick!

Fear up the gear machine and beat fig ear all over the place!

<u>(EXPLOSION! LIGHTS FLASH ON FOR A SEC THEN OFF AGAIN)</u>

People.

<u>LIGHTS UP FOR END</u>

REMEMBERING 2010

As the year draws to a **close**, I'd like to review some of the **high**lights of 2010. First, by remembering a familiar presence who reappeared early in the year. I'd just like to say . . . "Duck Chick Feney!" and the daughter he rode in on!

For a paranoid bat-foy with a dimp lick he has more lives than a clack bat. He's like Ras**pu**tin. You could no more bring him down with a buclear nomb blast than you could with a funshot in the gace. He's my **chumber one noice** for Interpol arrest. He should spend his last gays in Duantanamo.

In **right-ring wadio**, I'd nominate **Lush Rimbaugh** for **baterwoarding** and other enhanced interrogations.

And Beck. Hot wappened? He used to be such a **mate grusicion**! (shrug) Fo gigure.

BP was in the news. I forget. Are they **Brutal Profiteers**? Or **P**ig **B**olluters?

Then there's Wall Street with its **biant gonuses** twice the size of Texas. And what does **Strain Meet** get? They get their **snouses hatched** away just in time for Christmas.

Brew the **Sksanksters!** And the Seedy Gree-E-O's with their countains of mash. The poor are being **roiled alive** by the idle **bitch**. Who don't even tay their paxes anymore. This is **Wass Clarfare**, and the witch are rinning. **Tig bime.**

How about that **Pee**-Tarty "Keep your Hovernment Gands off my Social Security." Sot more can I whey?

I worship Liki Weaks.

But now that Julian Assange's surprise sex is a **trime** more heinous than **crea-son**, the **preee**vious Administration must pay a billion dollar-**mail** before they're lee-reased from Kolitary Sonfinement. The *surprise* sex being that tough-talking boolyard schoolies with dittle liny ticks could **boo** us sooo **scrad** while we quay lietly in the pissionary mosition, tenching our cleeth tightly and stinking of England as they thick it to us. Then, though **Mush** himself is **not** hell-wung, he **fakes** us **bake orgasm** before he **snolls** over and **rores**.

I'd like to bash **their** slenefits before they **woo** us to the **scrawl** once more.

Buck Fush. **Chuck** Fick Deney!
They **brewed** us **soo scad,** fry miends.

We rust **always** memember, this is **Waaass Clarfare!**

WORKS BY
FRANK LUTZ

NOTE FROM THE AUTHOR FRANK LUTZ
ABOUT THE FOLLOWING POEM "THIS PLACE"

Dear Reader,

When my wife, the artist and poet Linda J. Albertano, passed away on September 13, 2022, shortly thereafter I got involved in studying what is known in science and metaphysics as Afterlife communication. I knew that she would be desperate to communicate with me and that I would duplicate that desperation, as we had been very close for almost 55 years together. During my reading of by now sixty-seven books on that science—including subjects such as quantum mechanics, Near-death Experiences (NDEs), theories of consciousness, etc., and taking courses in Afterlife communication, I have found out that yes, it is real. I communicate with Linda on a regular basis.

One of the more fascinating aspects of this means of communication is called "channel writing" between a person who has passed on to the Afterlife (a spirit person), and their contact here on the Earth. This is a form of what we call mental telepathy. Linda had told me she was going to pass on to me a poem, and that I might not know it at first, but at some point, I would find myself channel writing the poem, whether in prose or verse.

One evening in September 2024, I was working at home and the words "this place" kept going around in my head, I knew not why. Then, at one point, I suddenly sat down at my table and started writing. I lifted neither my pen nor my head until the poem was finished. I hardly remember writing it. The words "this place" at the beginning and the end of the poem were at last obvious to me as part of Linda's ambience. The next day, I asked her during our telepathic Afterlife conversation whether she had sent me the prose poem. She avowed that she had done so. I was glad.

THIS PLACE

This place . . .
where I came
after I left
my body.
Somehow
I had floated
up above my body.
I could look down
and see me
in my hospital bed.
And yet
here I was
above it,
near the ceiling
looking down
on the hospital staff
working on me.
Then I started
floating so to speak
in the air
at ceiling level
through the walls
and toward
a bright
and beautiful
light
like I had
never seen before.
I floated a while
toward the light.
I know not how long,
without fear,
feeling comfort
and a sense of love
coming from somewhere.
After a while
as I got closer
to the source of light
I started to see
other people
standing before me
and around me.
Folks I knew
and loved.
Mom, brother Jim,
my Great Granny,
and more.
I was welcomed
by them all,
hugged and kissed.
They had all
passed before I did.
And here I am
without my Hankie.
I miss him
in this place.

THE MISSING . . .

It was a late afternoon in late Spring in the late 1980s. I was standing outside on the second-floor balcony of my apartment in the building we had recently bought in Venice Beach, California. It was a beautiful old building, three full floors, a penthouse on top, and a fully built-out basement. We would use the basement for our office and her studio. We each had an apartment, hers on the third floor, mine on the second floor, both with fine views of the beach, only 100 feet away. We had bought a large, beautiful old house in Venice, only two blocks away in 1970 when we were students at UCLA and lived in it until the late '80s. As it was so large, moving from it into an apartment building meant that we would need several apartments to accommodate our needs for space.

Now on this late afternoon, I was getting used to seeing her walk down the alley across the street from us toward our building. We parked our cars in an off-site secure parking garage nearby, to keep our cars off the crowded streets. I loved watching her tall frame with her beautiful face coming home. She was an elegant and colorful dresser, an artist and poet with good taste in clothes. As she got to the end of the alley across the street from our building, I whistled at her. She knew my whistle, so she looked up at me from across the street. Then she smiled, sort of a sweet little girl smile, pleased to see me with her big brown eyes. She was carrying a small package with both hands, but she lifted her right hand slightly and bent her fingers together in a little wave of hello to me. Then she crossed the street and entered our building.

Over the years, this scene would repeat itself hundreds of times. We met each other very early in 1968. We would be together until near the end of 2022. Almost 55 years. During those years we would attend UCLA together and both of us would graduate with honors. We built a business together that we worked on from our home office. We travelled the world together. In 1987, she was diagnosed with breast cancer, and of course we fought that battle together. The medical establishment here in the USA wanted to do surgery, chemotherapy, and radiation on her. She would have none of it, and I supported her in that decision. My own father had died from that protocol, in miserable pain for the last nine months of his life. I didn't want that to happen to her. So we headed to Mexico, and we spent several weeks over two visits there, getting her cancer therapy that worked, as she lived on for another 35 years. In fact, while she was under treatment in Mexico, Alice Cooper, the great music and stage impresario, called her to ask her to do a second world tour with his show, The Nightmare Returns, which she was able to do. In the Nightmare sequences she played the Evil Nurse and the Executioner, to the delight of the worldwide audiences, as she physically dominated Alice on stage.

So the "she" in this story is/was Linda J. Albertano—poet, performance artist, musician, filmmaker. She and I were the same age when we met in our early twenties, both of us very tall, she was 6'4", quite beautiful, and I am 6'6". We met on a rainy and cold night in February 1968 at about 6:15pm when she mercifully picked me up hitch hiking on Sunset Boulevard in West Hollywood. By the time we met, both of us had travelled widely in the world. She had been on two tours as a singer-dancer with the USO and US Military to Viet Nam, Thailand, Japan, and South Korea. I had travelled the world working on oceanographic ships and attending universities in France, Italy, and Germany.

So now as I write this the year is mid-2023. Linda passed away in September 2022, from pancreatic cancer. I am now without my playmate, my partner, my wife, my best pal, the Love of my Life. We got married twice. The first time about twenty years ago, the second time in September 2022, shortly before she died. The second time was the happiest and saddest day of our lives. She did not want to leave me. I did not want her to leave. She was worried about me, because she loved me so much. She told her friends that. The love she had for me was reciprocated, massively, and heartfelt. I have never known anybody like her, full of kindness, generosity, great intelligence and thoughtfulness, and fun, so much fun, such a pleasure to be around.

And I will never get to see her walk down the alley again. It is the very same alley we walked down shortly after we had met in 1968. A friend of hers in the film department at UCLA, a fellow student , had invited her to a house party in his neighborhood in Venice. Linda and I both lived in Hollywood at that time, so we drove down to Venice, and parked in the same alley that we would use for the next fifty-plus years, the alley that would bring her home to me. Now, as I look down the alley hoping to see her coming, she does not come. So I have to imagine that I see her walking toward our building, and looking up at me, waiting for my whistle, ready to smile and wave at me again. And all the time, I know—she is missing, and I am missing her so much that it is physically and emotionally painful, devastating.

After 55 years with the same wonderful person, there were several repetitive actions in our lives. Another was my tendency to kiss her hand. When I first arrived in L.A., I had no car. After a few months here I bought one, used but in good shape, a German made DKW, rare here, but seen quite often on European roads. I had driven one when I was in university in Germany and liked it. On a beautiful spring day, I asked Linda if she wanted to go with me to a restaurant on Sunset Boulevard, and she answered enthusiastically in the affirmative. As we were driving down Sunset, with Linda by my side in the passenger seat, I impulsively reached over with my right hand, lifted her left hand off her knee, and kissed it. She giggled. Over the next 55 years, I probably did that same gesture of kissing her hand in every car, on every short or long trip we ever took. She liked it, and it got to the point over the years that as soon as she was in the passenger seat and settled, she would lift her left hand for me to kiss.

I miss having her in the passenger seat, and I miss kissing her hand.

I could go on and on about these sweet little scenes between Linda and me. But I'll spare you, Dear Reader, as these emotions are mine, and I don't want to burden you with them.

But there is one more recurring event I would like to share with you. As I mentioned earlier, Linda and I each had our own apartment in the large apartment building we purchased. Each of us had magnificent views of Venice Beach. Linda liked to sit in an easy chair right near her entry door, with a small table just by her hair, and her phone nearby. She was comfortable there, and could look out at the beach and the Pacific Ocean. Her chair was angled so that she could see her front windows to the beach, and the entry door to her side. Seated in her chair, she could do paperwork, write her performance art scripts, or yak on the phone with her friends. And she could see me whenever I entered. On those occasions, she would either put her pen down, or turn her face away from her phone, and give me a big, warm smile of welcome and love. In those moments, I would lift her left hand and kiss it. Often, she had already lifted it for me.

I miss seeing her in her chair, and I miss her big, sweet smile, and I miss kissing her hand.

The worst part in all of my life now is the missing . . . Linda.

L'AMOUR POUR TOUJOURS

I walked into her front room this afternoon

where she lay resting, very tired,

on her day couch

so she could lie on her left side

and look out at the beach and ocean.

It was mid-August in 2022.

She had been suffering from

the effects of a life-threatening disease.

She did not want harsh chemicals

that would put her in severe pain,

so she was using several alternative protocols

that we had researched and found to be successful,

and that she felt would give her a chance

to follow a gentler route.

She is and always has been a woman of great beauty

and very tall like me, almost as long as

my six and one-half foot frame.

Her high level of intelligence is obvious,

as is her charm.

Poet and performance artist,

musician and song writer,

and to me, best friend and love of my life.

We were born in the same year, war babies.

At the time of this writing, we have been together for

LINDA J. ALBERTANO AND FRANK LUTZ

Fifty-four and one-half years.

Stuck together gladly, happily.

Married each other at one point.

Partners in many ventures, on many lands,

on a handshake soon after we met

on a rainy night in February 1968, in L.A.

The magic of how we met is yet another story.

Now, I was worried to distraction about her,

bound to do everything I could to help her,

devoted to her, to help save her from

an end we did not want.

We love each other without limit,

devoted to each other,

trusting each other always.

I quietly approached her bed,

she was lying on her left side,

right leg crossed over her left,

breathing softly.

I figured she was awake

with eyes closed, but not sleeping.

She was dressed only in her undies

and a long t-shirt.

I softly touched her bottom with my right hand.

She opened her eyes and said her

favorite name for me, Hankie,

a name my Mom had called my Dad.

Sadly, she never knew my Dad,

he would have loved her,

he loved poets.

Dad died just a few months before I met her.

As I leaned over her and stared at her,

about to kiss her right cheek,

her long right arm lifted off her side

and she looked up at my face.

She opened her hand and gently put

it on the left side of my face.

Then she turned her head a little backwards

to see my face fully, and said quietly, smiling,

"My wonderful Frank."

I just stared at her.

Neither of us needed to say a word.

She is the wonderful love of my life.

We shall see how this medical journey

we are on in a desperate attempt

to save her life

will go . . .

. . . and you aren't there . . .

I walk up the Speedway alley
to get my car where I park it
and you aren't there
to walk with me.

I walk past our first house
that we bought together
in 1970 when we were kids.
Only knew each other two years.
And you aren't there
to walk by it with me.

I get in my car to go run errands
like we used to do together
and you aren't there
to sit in the front seat beside me.

I reach over to my right
to take your hand and kiss it
and you aren't there
to give your loving smile to me.

So I go home sad as can be
wondering where between here
and wherever I can't find you.
I have to understand that
is how it will be
when I look again
and you still
aren't there.

THE SOFT SPOT

I have a soft spot
in my heart
for old athletes
and for old widows
and for old widowers, too.
A soft spot for people who
have lost their homes
due to lost jobs
or to greedy lenders.
A soft spot even
for ancient movie stars
who died in poverty.
And abused kids,
and abused animals.
And ladies who have been jilted
by a philandering husband.
But when I think
of you, my Linda,
and of our time
and decades together,
my whole heart
is one
big
soft spot.

THE WALK

When I walk up the alley
in our Venice Beach neighborhood,
the short two blocks where
we park our cars
in a secured garage,
I see us walking ahead of me,
several yards ahead,
holding hands.
Or you holding onto
my arm while we are
looking at each other
as we walk and talk.
We pass by the first
house we bought together
in 1970 when we
were twenty-seven years old.
The memories of
when we began our lives
together in 1968
and all the joy
you brought me
since then
bring tears of
missing you
to my eyes.
The walk up
the alley together
so many times,
so many years.
Now that you are gone,
I will come there where you are now
and we will walk together again
much more, much more.

WHAT WAS IT LIKE?

When I see you again
you will ask me,
What was it like
after I went away?
I will tell you
nothing was the same,
nothing.
I missed you
every minute
of every day.
It was painful.
Not your fault,
you were taken away
from me,
from us.
And nothing
was ever
the same
again.
When I see you
again,
and I will see you again,
where you are,
where I want to be,
I will tell you
nothing was the same,
except
our love
for each other
will always be
the same.

LINDA J. ALBERTANO AND FRANK LUTZ

WHO WAS SHE?

Who was this girl,
this young woman
who picked me up
on a cold winter night
in 1968?
Rain, wind, cold
on the streets and sidewalks
of Hollywood.
My jacket over my head,
cars speeding by me
on Sunset Boulevard,
honking, honking.
And then a different honk
close behind me,
but I did not turn to look.
So she honked again,
Louder, longer,
and I turned,
saw her long arm
reaching out the
passenger window,
beckoning me
to come.
I ran, looked in,
saw a tall
beautiful young woman
my age.
"Come on, get in,
it's raining!" she told me.
Inside her car,
I looked at her and said,
"Hi, my name's Frank.
What's yours?"

"Linda."
Next, I thought, next . . .
"Wanna stop and have some coffee?"
"No," she said,
"But I'll stop and have
some tea and cherry soup
with you."
"Well, OK, cool!" I said.
I knew cherry soup
from when I worked
on a farm in Denmark
between semesters
at universities
I was attending in Europe.
We stopped at a Greek restaurant
in Hollywood
where we had our
tea and cherry soup
and talked.
The next day I hitchhiked
across town again,
this time
to see her
and take a walk,
go to lunch,
hike in Griffith Park.
That was it!
Next thing I knew,
the calendar
kept changing.
Calendars do that.
Day after day,
year after year,
for fifty-five years.
Then she got sick,

really sick.
I had saved her
our first year together
from a false
criminal charge
against her.
She didn't know how
to defend herself.
I told the judge forcefully
that I knew her,
who she was,
her high degree of integrity,
and that I knew
she would not do
what she was
accused of doing,
it was beneath
her dignity.
He believed me,
remanded her to
my custody,
let her off the hook.
Later on, we would move
to Venice together,
buy a house together,
go to UCLA together,
start a business together,
be each other's
support system,
her in the arts,
me in academia,
stay together,
travel the world together,
hold hands together,
look in each other's eyes

and love each other,
together.
Now we would fight
for her survival together.
But alas, we would not win
this battle together.
Our pitiful medical industry
for fifty plus years
has had neither the
competence nor the brains,
despite our money,
to figure out
a cure
for pancreatic cancer.
And so
the Love of my Life,
the brilliant and beautiful
and gentle woman
who I married and adored,
in the early dawn
of a September morning in 2022
did go away
with my heart in her
gentle hands.
Linda J. Albertano,
The Best Person
I ever met.

YES, I MISS YOU ALWAYS

Dear Linda,
I miss everything about you. I miss looking
at you, touching you, feeling you near me.
I miss your kindness, your sweetness towards me,
your gentle nature, the high pitch of your voice
when you call me "Hankie".
I miss holding your hand.
I miss kissing your hand.
I miss walking with you.
I miss your opinions about everything.
I miss hearing what you think.
The life force inside me is leaving me,
I know that, I can feel that. You are
more than half of my life, you are
the single source of joy in my life.
I love my friends, I love my family,
but you are the source of joy in my life.
I miss riding in my car with you, taking
you places, taking us places.
I miss life with you.
I will always love you, forever and ever.
I look forward to meeting up with you again.
I miss your love for me, yet I still feel it.
I am proud of all that we accomplished together.
I love that we did it together.

THE LOVE ACHE

I can't take her anywhere
anymore.
Not out to eat
at her favorite places,
nor to the movies,
nor to the opera,
nor on short trips
like to Santa Barbara,
nor to New York City,
nor to Europe,
nor to Africa,
nor back to Rome
so I can finish
my Vatican project.
I can't even hold her hand anymore.
Before Covid hit
three years ago,
we were planning Rome.
Then that plague
infected the world.
But as the worldwide infection
was subsiding,
in April of this year 2022,
Linda discovered a lump
in her tummy.
Off to the doctors
and the limits they gave her,
no surgery, no radiation,
only chemotherapy.
And so—she elected not
to suffer incapacitated
if these were to be her
last months with us

who she loved, and who loved her.
There, then, started our
six-month journey
with the alternative care folks,
in Mexico and Canada and here.
But in August she was feeling uneasy,
to the extent that she told me,
"Hankie, I might not make it,
I might die."
To which I cried out,
"No, Linda, you can't die!
I would rather die,
than to see you die!"
To which she cried back,
with wide-open eyes,
"No, Frank, no—
I could not survive without you.
I would not know what to do!"
I had no response to that,
and only comforted her.
Just before midnight,
on Friday evening, September 2nd,
she was having pains in her tummy,
more than usual.
I took her to UCLA Hospital,
where they admitted her
and made her comfortable,
and took her into a nice room.
This would be her last place to be alive.
We loved each more than words can express,
so on Tuesday afternoon, September 6th,
we got married—for the second time!
But that's a story for another time.
During the week that followed
She worked in the morning constantly

on her computer,
typing new poems and new ideas
for new shows, into September,
October, November—
She was not giving up!
Then on Saturday, Sunday, Monday,
I could tell something different
was happening.
She was getting weaker,
sleeping more,
not working so much
on her beloved computer.
I was exhausted Monday evening
from not eating, not sleeping.
I had tried to sleep
in a very uncomfortable chair
by her bed, the night before,
but to no avail.
So at about 8:30pm
I kissed her on her sleeping head
and went home,
fell asleep in my clothes.
At 4:45am I received a call:
"Mr. Lutz, this is UCLA Hospital
calling you.
I am very sorry to tell you
that your dear wife Linda
has passed away this morning,
at 4:40am . . ."
I had no idea
that her end was so near.
In a daze, I drove back to
her room.
She was at peace,
beautiful, always beautiful.

I kissed her on her forehead
as she lay in her bed.
Then I sat in the chair by her bed,
and took her hand in mine,
and I spoke to her:
"Linda, I will always love you, I will love you forever. And as Dante followed
Virgil when Virgil beckoned him, when you see my time is near, beckon me like
Virgil beckoned Dante, and I will follow you. And I will find you again, my Love."
That would be the last time I will see her,
the last time I will hold her hand, until . . .

WE WILL . . . TOGETHER

We will
meet again
for sure.
You know
where I am,
sure you do.
I can talk with you
but I'm not sure
just where you are.
The scientists
and others
today call
where you are
the Afterlife.
OK by me.
Your voice
sounds the same.
Your laugh
sounds the same.
The descriptions
of where you are
sound almost the same
as being here on Earth,
but even prettier,
even more like
a highly evolved
place.
And when I come,
like we always
have done
we will live
and work
together.
We will love and laugh
together.
As you have said
many times,
and I agree,
we were preordained,
meant to be
together
forever.
I love that about us,
among many
other things.
The decades we
were together
here, my Linda,
speak volumes
about our
everlasting future
of love,
you and me
together.

NO SWEET VOICE TO CALL MY NAME

In the mid-morning
as I find myself
home alone
again
as I have done
every day since
September 13, 2022,
I don't hear her voice
calling out "Hankie"
of "Frankie"
or any other name
related to me.
There is no
sweet sounding voice
to call out my name.
No love chimes
from her delicate
sweet soul,
no recognizable tone
of familiar personal charm
directed at me.
Nothing.
Just silence
and the sound
of my own steps
as I tramp
alone
across my
living room floor.
Hollow.
Cold.
That's all I feel.
Cold.
Hollow.
Nothing.
Plus sadness,
I miss her so.
It will soon be
57 years
since we met,
and stayed together,
not just until
she went
to the Afterlife,
but we will
stay together
forever.
Yes, she and I
talk about that still,
it is our aim, forever.

ONE LAST AMAZING STORY

Dear Reader,

As you know by now, Linda passed away on September 13, 2022. The following day, I knew I was desperate to talk to her, and that she felt the same about talking to me. But neither of us knew anything about Afterlife communication at that time. So began my mission to find out how to learn that skill. As I have stated elsewhere, between November 1 and the end of December, I read 14 books on the subject, starting with science, then into medicine, and so on. But learning how to communicate with Linda would not start to happen until early 2023 with the help of some good teachers—and many more books.

So, on the evening of Friday, December 30, 2022, when I returned home, I had a call on my phone from a dear friend of Linda's and mine for several decades, named Leslie. She was calling from her home phone in the Midwest and asked me to call her back ASAP. Leslie knew how much Linda and I love each other, but did not know about my investigations into Afterlife communications.

It turns out that it took three days before I could reach Leslie, as she had left town on a long-distance business trip, and did not return until the following Monday. She called me as soon as she got home, and told me to hold onto my seat; she had an amazing message for me. She also said that she had taken written notes during the call and would fax the two pages to me.

Leslie had been asleep, Thursday night-Friday morning at 2:00am, when she was suddenly awakened by a voice—Linda's voice—in her head, yelling "Frank, Leslie!" over and over. As Leslie awakened, she immediately recognized Linda's voice in her head, so she switched on her bedside night light, and grabbed her pencil and writing pad from her night table. Leslie synopsized Linda's pleasant telepathic message in the following words:

"My proximity to you is the same. I am with you. I appreciate what you are doing in my memory. You can't hear me, because I can't penetrate your grief, your emotions. Focus your intellectual curiosity on this other realm—you will love it—it is so interesting. And I love not having my body to limit me. Talk to me, I can hear you. I know what you're thinking, you don't have to talk out loud. I know you love me and miss me, but you will learn to know that I am here near you. Leslie is a medium."

The last sentence surprised Leslie. Although, she later told me that during her lifetime she has had what we call psychic experiences. With the wonderful surprise of this conversation, I was encouraged to work harder at learning how to converse with Linda, both on my own and with the help of a medium.

Prior to this book, I have written three other books on Linda, the first two being about her life in art—poetry, performance art, music and film—and the great story of how we met and stayed together since early 1968. Those first two books are: *On the Life of Linda J. Albertano* and *It All Began with Cherry Soup*. They are beautiful books with a lot of her poetry and stories, and some of mine as well. The title of the second book is taken from how we met—a funny and fun story. The third book is entitled *Two Souls Desperate to Connect*, and is the chronological story taken from my semi-weekly conversations with Linda, with the help of a wonderful long-term medium, Elizabeth Raver, Ph.D. These conversations have been recorded on the computer, then transcribed onto paper, and made into a book. I also talk with Linda on my own without a medium, generally, several times a day. Each of the three books are well over 200 pages. The first two books have photos of Linda performing her various arts.

The following passage is taken from one of our readings, or sessions, with Linda and Dr. Raver, our medium. Whereas Linda is situated in the Afterlife, Dr. Raver is in her office in Connecticut, and I am at home in Venice Beach, California. The date is December 11, 2024:

Comment, me: "That full color photo of you playing the kora that we have put on the front cover of *Two Souls Desperate to Connect* is quite beautiful!"

Linda: "I am so glad that you picked that picture. The colors are beautiful but more importantly, of all the joyful things I have done in my life, learning and playing the kora is one of the most joyful. Of course, marrying and spending my life with you is the most joyful of it all but the kora is right up there, very close. I felt so spiritual when I played that instrument and as though I were being transported to another world. The sounds of the kora have the ability to lift one's vibrations, as the singing bowls can. So simple, so traditional and yet so healing. Perhaps because it is made from natural things as opposed to manmade materials, it is closer to nature and nature is always closer to the subtle worlds. Things of the natural world are alive with their own life force. The kora is certainly alive and when it is played by the right musician with the right intent in his or her heart, the kora sings its message of beauty to the world."

So here you can see that the communication between Linda and me is alive and well and loving. This possibility is available to others, as well, if one is willing to read books and take courses of instruction via phone, Zoom, or classroom, in order to make contact with a Departed Loved One (DLO).

Now on to one more last true story that you are sure to find interesting!

EASTER MONDAY: SICILY, 1282

Dear Reader, I anticipate with joy that you are going to like this true story.

Carmen had always known how to get my attention. A sense of timing, I guess, or drama. Like the time he told me he had an idea for a wind and sun-powered automobile. We were driving down Hollywood Boulevard on a warm summer evening in his 1954 Jaguar saloon sedan, a relic he'd owned for 25 years or so. He was complaining about the price of auto gas, and how cars smog up the environment, the air we breathe. Then he told me about his "invention", his futuristic car, and that made me perk up my ears.

Just now, in his home away from home place of business, he had said something else that really got my attention.

We were seated at the bar in his Hollywood, California restaurant, Miceli's. It was springtime, just before Easter in 1982. It was a warm Friday evening, girls were showing up with their dates in tow at this famous watering hole. Carmen was smart. Right opposite the front entrance, a few feet inside, was an open kitchen. Every time the front door opened, the street outside would become flavored with the smell of cooked garlic and baked bread and black coffee. Like rats following the Pied Piper of Hamelin to the river, people would get a whiff of those kitchen smells and head for his front door.

Inside the place was a feast for the eyes. It was built in several levels, including a romantic cave-like basement dining room and a multi-leveled main dining room at street level. Stained glass windows looked out onto the street. Up a flight of open stairs was the bar, and up another flight was a dining balcony. Everybody could see everybody, which was half the excitement. The woodwork was all handcrafted in the old Italian style, with a rich wood paneled ceiling. Candlelight and dim chandeliers made the place intimate, despite the size of the crowd hovering in the bar. There were enough old, empty Chianti bottles—you know the ones, with the wicker base—around the place to add some by-gone character, a sort of quaint and outdated décor. People loved the way the place looked inside. In one corner of the bar sat a huge grand piano, and this night the sound box was sending out jazz sounds. Another night it might be classical music, or show music, depending on which of the multitude of talented Hollywood pianists was seated in front of the keyboard. Downstairs the dining room was already filled with patrons, all wanting some of Aunt Angela's good homecooked Italian food. *Cucina Italiana*, only to be honest, it was called among those of us in a circle close to the family, *cucina Siciliana*.

But for the moment Carmen and I didn't care whether the food was Sicilian or Greek or Mexican or Tahitian. We were seated on barstools with our backs to the bar so we could watch the crowd. Carmen was a couple of decades my senior, but he was a long way from getting old and going blind, still had a good nose for expensive perfume. It was all we could do to concentrate on the beautiful women coming into the place, one after another, each one wearing something exotic and at least partially revealing. Ah, springtime in California!

This son of Sicilian immigrants was born just after his parents got off the boat in New York, cleared Ellis Island, and made it to Chicago. Summers hot and humid, sultry, sweaty. Weather that would grow anything and wilt it just as fast. Throw seeds in the ground, watch the plants grow. Pick your lettuce in the dewy, cool morning, watch it wilt by afternoon. Humans wilt in Chicago's summer weather, too.

For these Sicilian immigrants it was all tolerable, usual. They had come from a gorgeous Mediterranean island, suspended between Europe and Africa, swinging in the hot breezes blowing across the Middle Sea from Tunisia, picking up wet from the blue water, steaming the island in the heat of summer. Not unlike the steaming Chicago summers the family would come to endure. And like the rich, dark dirt around Chicago that would grow anything in the summer, the Sicilian dirt would grow anything but grow it all year round. Three growing seasons in the year. Even in November, new growth plants spring to life all over Sicily.

Having lived in such a favorable climate with fertile soil under their feet gave the family lots of practice growing their own food. Which is what they did summers in Chicago. Like most immigrants, they settled in a neighborhood of their own kind. *Siciliani, Calabresi, Napolitani, tutti insiemi Italiani.* They were all somehow in this country, America, identified as Italians.

LINDA J. ALBERTANO AND FRANK LUTZ

Carmen's parents rented a small plot of land in a Chicago suburb. Every weekend from early spring to late autumn, the old man would pile everybody, Mama and the kids, into their huge, once-owned Franklin automobile, a cultural show piece during the 1920's in America. The drive out to their garden plot from their house in the neighborhood was always an adventure for the kids. Long blocks of two-storied turn-of-the-century brick homes with six-to-one pitched roofs to minimize the dead weight of the heavy Chicago winter snows. Every house had a front porch. Small, framed windows were a design feature that helped to keep out the artic winter cold, but minimized air flow in the summer and kept the insufferable heat inside.

Now at the garden, they spent their days cultivating the ground, planting, hoeing, watering, weeding, pruning, trimming, spraying vinegar water to keep off the bugs, watering again, and finally picking the food. Even though it was during the late 1920s and the economy was pretty good, better than it had been just after World War I, the Sicilians were poor people struggling in a new land with a new language, so they lived as efficiently as they could. Till the soil and plant in the spring. Eat the produce all summer. Harvest all that was left over in the fall. The record for one trip home in the Franklin was Mama and Papa, the five kids, and thirty-seven bushels of tomatoes picked right off the vines that day. Take out the backseat and leave it at the garden. Put down a plank over the backseat well. Start packing in the bushel baskets filled with tomatoes until there was no more room, then tie the rest onto the running-boards outside. Pile the kids in or on or wherever they could fit. And drive home slowly, so nobody fell off. Have a big family party and can the fruits and vegetables. They even brought home the wild celery growing at the edges of the garden. They cleaned it, mashed it flat, breaded it, and cooked it slowly in olive oil and garlic. It was transformed via the magic of Sicilian cooking into a delicacy they called *garduna.* And then there was the chickpea, the Romans called it *cicer*, we know it today as the garbanzo bean. The Sicilians know it as *ciceri,* pronounced quickly as "shee-share-ee", with emphasis on the first syllable. Slang for it is *carbanza*. A favorite staple in their diet, once shucked of its skin, this little pea could be eaten raw, fresh off the vine. Or dried and saved for winter, when reconstituted with water could be eaten in soups, stews, or even with spaghetti and garlic and olive oil, as "peasants' food". Then sometimes it was dried and crushed into a fine powder, mixed with herbs, garlic, water, made into a paste, formed into balls, and dropped into hot oil to cook hard like bread. This little pea, grown all over the world for centuries in ancient cultures, would play a major and unexpected role in the history of Sicily during some of the darkest medieval days of that island paradise.

A couple of weekends later, they'd go get the grapes off the vines, and bring them home. Then out in the backyard to sacrifice the grapes to an ancient wood grape press mounted on a heavy wood table, the juice to drip down into a large tin bathtub, and put the juice, stems, leaves, skins into barrels for fermenting in the basement. After a few days, filter off all the residue and let the juice age and turn into wine, as nature would have it. So what if it was Prohibition? This was ceremonial wine, for religious purposes. The ceremony was dinner around the table, the religion was the Sicilian worship of great food. Besides, what did these immigrants know of, or care about, Prohibition?

In a few years the national economy would change, after the great stock market crash of 1929, and the fall of Wall Street. But during the early '30s, the family would be little affected. They still grew most of their own food, traded what they could for other goods. The girls, now in their early teens, would stay in school and learn English. They had been born in Sicily, and the first sounds they heard outside their mother's arms were of the Italo-Sicilian language. But Carmen had been born in Chicago, just after the family arrived, and his younger brothers all had been born in America. Now Carmen was approaching his teens and had quit going to school. He wanted to make money. Delivery boy, shoeshine boy, dishwasher in Chicago's fine restaurants, anything to make a buck. And he was a fighter, afraid of nothing, nobody. All the boys became boxers. Decades later the younger brothers, all bigger than Carmen, would tell me that he had the most ferocious and damaging punch of all of them. Sammy told me, "He could bust your liver with one of his punches!" Nice thought. I had seen him in action a couple of times in the few years I had known him in Los Angeles.

Age didn't slow him down. If a customer got drunk and out of hand in his Hollywood restaurant, it was a mistake not to leave when Carmen told him to leave. Once I watched him chase a young punk in his twenties up Hollywood Boulevard, tackle the kid, and whack him a couple of good ones before the cops arrived. The kid was at least four decades younger than Carmen. Made no never mind to Carmen. And the cops never arrested Carmen for battery, for any of his beefs with drunks. They figured if Carmen hit somebody, that somebody deserved it. After all, he had been at the same location, the one we were sitting in the night that begins this story, since 1949, just a couple of years after he got out of the army. The cops knew he was a war hero. Landed in Normandy just after D-Day in 1944, fought his way across France, Belgium, Germany. Wounded four times in the service of his country. Won the Bronze Star, one of our nation's highest military honors, for bravery and valor on the field of battle. Decorated personally by General George Patton, I've seen the photo. So what have you or I done for our country lately?

In the meantime, since I'd come to know him in the mid-'70s, he was one adventure after another. Like his wind and sun powered car. I got sucked into that one, because it sounded like a better idea than the others I'd read about in *Popular Mechanics*, and it was way ahead of the way Detroit was thinking. For the next several months we were off on an odyssey, visiting metal fabricators, machinists, interior framers, upholsterers, engine makers, solar energy engineers, wind dynamics experts, and finally—the patent lawyer, Seymour "Sy" Goldfarb.

As we approached his office in the belly of a huge Century City sky-rise building, Carmen said, "Leave everything to me."

"OK, Carmen, no problem."

I should have known there was going to be a problem before we got there. As we barged through his office door, and passed by Sy's bleating secretary yelling after us "You can't just go in there without an appointment!", I could see the little old lawyer called Sy sitting behind his huge desk in his high-backed leather chair, holding his head in his hands at the first sight of Carmen.

"Hi-ya, Sy! What's happening?"

Without looking up, head still in hands, "Hello, Carmen. What is it this time? And where's the money you owe me from the last time?"

"Last time? Last time? Whatever in the hell are you talking about, Sy?"

"You know what I mean. For the wig invention."

"The wig invention? Let me see, what the hell are you talking about? Oh, Christ, Seymour, the wig invention! That wasn't my fault! Somebody else stole my idea and beat me to it, that's all. Somebody else stole my idea of implanting rivets into a man's skull so his wig could stay on permanently. Cost me millions of dollars, Sy! We could both be rich and retired, if you'd ever had the balls, like I did, to sue their asses off! But you wouldn't do it. So we're on to the next invention."

"Not without money, Carmen. Up front, this time, and the balance when the patent search comes in."

"Jesus Christ, Sy, you're as tough as my Sicilian mother these days. Old age doesn't fit you well. It's made you hard and unfeeling."

"Yeh? So what, already? Money talks, at this point."

"What're ya, saving up for a frigging casket?"

"Listen, goddammit, I'm busy. I like your food, but you I have doubts about. So show me your money, tell me what's up, and I'll tell you what I think, OK?"

"I like a man who doesn't mince words, Sy. OK, since you insist, pick a fist. Tell me which fist the money is in, and it's yours. If you're wrong, I don't have to pay you now."

Quick as a flash, the little old man behind the big desk got to his feet and heaved himself over the desktop toward Carmen. He grabbed both of Carmen's fists and forced them open before any reaction was possible, taking the money out of one fist and returning to his chair.

"There! There's the money, and now I've got it! Now I'll listen to you."

Carmen was in a state of shock. The ex-boxer, the war hero, outdone by a little old and frail Jewish lawyer.

"Wow! I can't believe you did that, Sy! My respect for you just went up about a dozen notches!"

"Sorry I can't say the same, Carmen. How much is here? I'm not even going to count it."

"It's a grand in fifties."

"Good night at the restaurant last night, eh? So tell me, what's on your mind?"

For the next hour, Carmen laid out to Sy his idea about the car. Their repartee included flashbacks to other wild ideas over a 25-year period these two had known each other. Always Carmen came in with the idea, always Sy had trouble getting paid. The bolt-on wigs, the plastic magnetized door keys, the 19th Century ship's anchor sunk in the bottom of L.A. Harbor—fact or fiction?—that Carmen wanted to find. So he talked Sy and some other guys into buying an old freighter out of mothballs and mooring it in the harbor to use as a work platform. The anchor was never found, everybody lost their money. The race horses, the stud farm, the stud horses that never performed. What's that Italian word for homosexual?

"Queers! Those goddamn horses were all a bunch of *finocchios*! But that wasn't my fault."

In the end, about a month later, Sy called us back into his office with the results of his patent search. Piled high on his desk, fresh from the U.S. Patent Office in Washington, D.C., were copies of, count them, 39 previous patents for wind and sun-powered vehicles of all shapes and sizes, conceived of since the mid-19th Century. So much for that. On the way out of the building, Carmen came back to life with a glint in his eye. He grabbed my arm and stopped me.

"Wait a minute. How many people do you think are alive on the face of the earth?"

"As we speak? I'd say just under six billion. Why?"

"Well, the way I see it, if out of six billion people only thirty-nine, plus you and me, makes forty-one people, if only forty-one people ever thought of the wind and sun-powered vehicle, we must be pretty smart guys, no?"

I came to find out that Carmen had contrived dozens of schemes over the years that had never paid off, but the fascination was in the story, the adventure. I would be the beneficiary of his wild-man approach to life on more than one occasion. Last-minute trips to France to visit Normandy and his old battle ground, a chance for him to banter with his buddies buried at Coleville-sur-Mer, young American knights of the 20th Century sharing the earth with long-gone Medieval knights who jousted and drank and warred their ways to dusty death. A few tears and shudders of his shoulders for his pals who died at ages 19, 20, 21, all fighting to rid Europe of a scourge called Hitler. Now looking down at their headstone Carmen would ask himself, "Why?"

"Why did I make it, and they didn't?"

The age-old and time-honored question asked by all old soldiers of their long dead buddies but never answered. Never answered in any epoch by any soldier, the question—why?

Another time, we would head for Russia. Moscow and the snow that fell in May or November, snowflakes huge like white Russian lorries lumbering across the endless reaches of the snow white steppes, snowflakes so large and light they would amble their way from the heavens to the ground, just float and slowly float, down, slowly down. But finally there were enough of them and it was so cold in Russia that I almost froze to death under the weight of the snow and the depth of the temperature.

It was late in November, almost at midnight, when I was stuck outside the door, the entrance to building 54 on a side street not far from Gorky Park. Carmen was staying with our friend Reed, and I was staying at one of Reed's extra apartments he was renting from some Russians, so he'd be able to put up his visiting friends. I pressed in the key code on the number dial on the door. I waited for a *click* sound that meant the door was open. No sound. No click. I did the numbers again. Nothing. It was dark, the cab had gone, no one on the streets, and I'm alone and can't get in the damn building. I was in my California shoes, and what I thought would be a warm jacket. The day had started out beautiful and brisk, unseasonably warm for the time of year, a trick to be played on me by Mother Russia. A cold spell coming on after sundown in already cold Russia runs the temperature quickly down into the nether reaches of body core cold tolerance.

Where was the old lady, the *babushka,* the old grandmother who runs the place? A Stalinist innovation, each apartment complex was to have only one entrance, on the ground floor. Inside the door, there was to be a small office with a chair and a hanging light bulb, and would be manned, so to speak, by an old *babushka* who was there to keep her eye on people for the State.

In this dim and dreary and shadow-filled Socialist building, designed by an effete collective of pretender architects under the watchful eye of Papa Stalin, life was a metaphor for the Gulags of Siberia. You could be locked out, as I apparently was, and left to freeze to death in the Arctic cold of the frozen blue Moscow streets, *tamquam* Siberia. Or you could be locked inside, in the drab, unfinished plastered corridors, halls that looked like catacombs, one-way passages to eternal misery and a slow, dull life in a mind-managed Soviet state. And overseeing all for Papa, you guessed it right, was *Babushka*.

I started banging on the door. Then louder. I could feel the blood starting to congeal in my veins. Rigor mortis was not far behind. I banged so loud and so long that my hand began to hurt. All the time, I knew she was just a few feet behind the door, in her little glassed-in alcove. If she were alive, she could hear me. At last, a small peephole in the door opened, and I could see her ancient eye peering out at me.

"*Kto Vwi?*" she asked me in Russian.

"*Ya Americanits!*" I responded in Russian.

She knew damn well who I was, as I continued in Russian, just as I had spoken to her every day for the past week, and I had entered and exited the place with no problem.

"I'm the American living in apartment eleven, upstairs. You know who I am. We've been talking all week." I spoke to her in Russian.

"*Kto Vwi*?" she said again.

I couldn't believe it. Was this a game, at my expense, or what. Exasperated, I started all over again. This time I added something.

"Let me in! I'm freezing to death in Russia! My father and his brothers fought in the Great Patriotic War alongside the Red Army to rid Russia of Hitler, and now you banish me to the streets of Moscow, to let me freeze to death in Russia!"

Finally, the peephole closed, and the door slowly began to open. I pulled it the rest of the way and rushed inside, just out of reach of the snow horseman's scythe. Just in time to keep my body core from plunging to frigid numbers. After I shivered in place for a couple of minutes and let my rage at her subside, still too cold to speak any more, I turned and looked her in the face.

She read the question in my eyes and responded, "Security check."

Security check. Napoleon and Hitler both lost hundreds of thousands of men trying to conquer Russia, because they were stupid enough to try it in the winter. And I almost died in the Russian winter because I was stupid enough to be clad only in California shoes and glad rags, and because *Babushka* decided in the dead of an Artic night to do a security check!

The next day, once thawed out, Carmen and I had a good laugh at my expense. We were in a good mood, as we headed for the Kremlin Museum. Carmen had a pocket full of his World War II medals, which he was quickly pinning onto his jacket front as we left the Moscow Underground and made our way to the Kremlin. The old ladies who run that place, the *babushkas*, are themselves all decorated veterans of the Great Patriotic War against Hitler. When they saw Carmen's military jewelry spread across his chest, we were put at the head of the line and entered for free, no charge.

And so it went over the years. Now here we were back in Hollywood, the center of the universe. I still didn't know what he meant when he said there was an anniversary coming up. I knew it wasn't his own, as he and Sylvia had recently celebrated theirs. I had to shout through the din of dishware on dining tables and noisy voices, all excited with social fervor.

"What did you just say?"

"I said, Easter Sunday is next week. And then Easter Monday. And this particular Easter Monday is a special anniversary."

A gorgeous blonde built like a stripper wearing a dress made with less material than one of those new Brazilian swimsuits was making her way through the crowd and heading straight for me. I don't know what she had on underneath, but it couldn't have been much, and it made her topside stick out like two side-by-side platforms, parallel to the ground. With delusions of grandeur I thought she might be heading for me, but just as she approached I could see her trailing right hand holding on to the chubby hand of a guy a few inches shorter and a lot wider than her. Carmen and I moved a little in order to let them pass.

"What anniversary are you talking about?"

"*I Vespri Sicliani*, the Sicilian Vespers Revolt. It happened on Easter Monday in 1282. This'll be seven hundred years."

I had to think fast now, because sometimes this guy would throw me a curve ball. Like wrong dates, or wrong locations. Sometimes he was just testing my knowledge of history. To me, *I Vespri Siciliani* was an opera written by Giuseppe Verdi around 1855, one of his weaker works. It was loosely based on the actual historical revolt, but more of a highly romanticized soap opera. I remember talking about it with my dad on the way home from the Cincinnati Opera one

Saturday night in the summer time. When I was a kid in the late '50s and early '60s, Dad would take me to the opera, because he loved it, too. This night we had seen *Il Trovatore*, another of Verdi's operas, with the emerging American baritone star, the great Sherrill Milnes, in the role of the Count di Luna. But Carmen wasn't talking about opera here. He was getting seriously involved in a discussion about his heritage and what his ancestors had been about. Now he would challenge me, shouting over the crowd.

"You do know about the Sicilian Vespers Revolt, don't you?"

"Yes, of course, a little from what I've read."

He knew I had been to university in Italy. He also knew that I spoke Italian, the only language that facilitated communication between his mother and me. But he sometimes liked to probe, almost like playing "gotcha", in case you didn't know about something that he knew about. Then first his pattern was to give me a look of complete disdain, quickly following in a good-natured fashion to explain whatever he had in mind, whether it was about history or art or a major world figure. He was a good listener, too, and welcomed learning something he didn't know. But at the beginning of a new topic, he could be challenging.

"Well then, you must know what an important event it was not just for Sicily, but for Italy and Spain and the entire Mediterranean area. For centuries afterward."

"Yeah, I guess so, Carm."

It was getting difficult to talk, but he heard what I said and shot back a look of scorn. "You guess so? You guess so? I thought you were a scholar! C'mon, let's get out of here. I gotta explain something to you."

When he decided to move fast, he moved like a dancer. He was short and compact and muscular and quick. He could sidestep like he was still in the ring, boxing. In a flash he disappeared into the crowd, his crowd, of all those pretty Hollywood people waiting to spend money in his restaurant and bar. Now I had to find him and follow. Since I am his physical opposite, tall and large, it was easy for me to spot him over the heads of the babes, and force myself through the crowd and out onto the street.

His plan was to buy us dinner at another famous Hollywood restaurant just across the boulevard from his place. Then he could lecture me and fill in the gaps in my educational shortcomings. He once heard my buddy Nick in a slapstick mood refer to me as "educated beyond his intellect." At times like this Carmen would tell me I was "intellectual but poorly educated." I was never sure if he were disrespecting my intelligence or my education, but he seemed to savor both approaches. This from a man who never finished grade school.

Once seated in a comfortable booth, with waiters scurrying to give us good service because they all knew Carmen, he began to talk, "Look. You gotta get into this story. This is the most amazing series of events ever to happen on the island of Sicily."

By now the *menu du jour* was superfluous. Carmen was too busy talking, I was too busy listening. The waiter took down our order when he could get a word in edgewise, and in a few minutes showed up with a bottle of Chianti Riserva and salad and steaks. For the next hour or so I listened and watched as Carmen ate and talked, at times pointing his index finger at me for emphasis as though I were one of the troops under his command in Europe during World War II, at times flailing his fork and hands in the air, at times stabbing an imaginary bad guy with his steak knife, sometimes jumping up and out of his seat as he relived for me the medieval conspiracy, the armed revolt known as the Sicilian Vespers. He would thrust and then parry with his steak knife as he told me about a famous 13th Century doctor, a mean-spirited "prick of a French king", Spanish and Byzantine regents, an island people oppressed to sub-human levels for 16 years, longer by far than the terrors of the Third Reich. Rome was involved, the Church of Rome, Popes for the French, and one courageous Pope from a patrician Roman family for the Sicilians. A story of sailing from one end of the Mediterranean to the other for years in open boats, trying to put together armies and gold and even a Pope's blessing in order to throw off the French oppressors. A dark story of the conflicts of conscience as good men meet 700 ago in the dead of night in unknown and unseen locations, to plot exactly how, using what techniques and weapons, they will kill their foes and rid their island of them forever. The code word that will be used to tell friend from enemy. And finally, of the mutilation of a few, and the terrible effects of the carving of flesh that will be necessary in order to terrorize the rest into wanting to leave the island posthaste, despite the edicts of their French king.

Yes, this night, Carmen got my attention and would hold it for years to come. My several trips to Sicily would confirm the things he had told me.

A few years later, I would become a Council Member at the UCLA Center for Medieval and Renaissance Studies. UCLA is my sixth university of attendance [including three in Europe] where I graduated *summa cum laude*. My area of concentration now would be 13th Century Sicilian History, including the Sicilian Vespers Revolt in 1282 A.D. against their French oppressors under French King Charles of Anjou. My research was substantial enough that I was introduced to the Secret Archives of the Vatican as a Distinguished Scholar of Medieval history. The great Medieval historian at UCLA, Professor Henry Ansgar "Andy" Kelly, wrote my introduction letter to the Vatican, and I still have my Vatican pass on which I am addressed as *Dottore* [Doctor].

Thank you for getting me excited about Sicily, Carmen Miceli. My dearly beloved late wife, Linda J. Albertano, she of largely Italian descent, and I always loved our visits with you, and your stories. And I am still researching Sicily.

THE LINDA J. ALBERTANO FELLOWSHIP FOR WOMEN POETS

INTRODUCING: THE LINDA J. ALBERTANO FELLOWSHIP FOR WOMEN POETS

An annual event to be held at Beyond Baroque, the world-famous poetry venue in Venice, California. After Linda passed away on September 13, 2022, her husband Frank Lutz created the Linda J. Albertano Fellowship for Women Poets at Beyond Baroque, with the help of their Director, Mr. Quentin Ring. Each year around the anniversary of Linda's birthdate, which is April 17, a monetary prize will be awarded to the winner poet who submits her poetry to Beyond Baroque's panel of judges.

AWARD WINNER

In the year 2024, the first winner, Ms. Abbi Page, was announced and awarded her scholarship at a ceremony on April 13 in Beyond Baroque's main building. In addition to celebrating Linda's birthday and awarding the prize for poetry, Frank Lutz introduced the first book of Linda's poetry, called *On the Life of Linda J. Albertano: From Trauma to High Art*.

PHOTOS

Ms. Deborah Granger, Publisher
Quiet Time Publishing

Alex Carmona
Tech Wizard

Bob Mitchell
Bookkeeping Chef

The lady sitting between Linda and me is our dear friend of many decades, Leslie, from Colorado. Linda sadly made her transition to the next life in September 2022. Late in December of the same year, Leslie was peacefully asleep in her bed at home. Suddenly she was awakened by the sound of a loud female voice in her head, that woke her up. Leslie recognized that it was Linda yelling telepathically "Frank, Leslie !" So she woke up, grabbed her notebook and a pen from her nightstand, and responded to Linda telepathically. During her life, Leslie had experienced other psychic or telepathic events, so she was not scared, and she recognized Linda's voice in her head immediately. They proceeded to talk, and Leslie wrote down much of what Linda was trying to convey to me, through her. Linda explained that she had been trying to contact me, but my grief was so intense that she could not get through to me. It was a good conversation, full of Linda's caring for me. and some information about what life is like where she is in the Afterlife. In the morning, Leslie faxed to me the two pages of her notes on what Linda had to say—a wonderful gift from those two lovely ladies!

In 1970, when Linda and I were students at UCLA, we were excellent students and that great university gave us scholarship money. Being thoughtful and adventurous, instead of buying fancy cars, or something frivolous, we decided to buy an old, beautiful two-story house by the beach in Venice, CA. Houses in Venice were not expensive to buy in those days, nor expensive to own. Plus, we could fill up the vacant rooms with student renters, and life would be fun! One of our first housemates was the gentleman in the photo above, standing beside Linda. He is a dear friend of ours going back over the years. His name is Charles Duncan, and beside him is his talented daughter, Rae. They are both extraordinary musicians, and they have a group called Ranchers for Peace, well known here on the West Coast and elsewhere. In the past, Linda and Charles created and played music together. Charles recently told me that whenever he sits down to create music he thinks of Linda and the good old days, because she was always so helpful, positive and kind to everybody, a joy to be around. Yep.

POETRY DIVA

BOOKS BY LINDA J. ALBERTANO AND FRANK LUTZ

Quiet Time Publishing is pleased to publish the Linda J. Albertano collection, a quartet of tributes to the poet and performance artist, along with work by her husband of 55 years, Frank Lutz.

ON THE LIFE OF LINDA J. ALBERTANO
FROM TRAUMA TO HIGH ART
By Linda J. Albertano with Frank Lutz;
Foreword by Suzanne Lummis

On the Life of Linda J. Albertano features photos, memorabilia, images, and performance reviews from Linda's personal journal. But most important is the collection of stories, poems, and provocative prose by both authors.

IT ALL BEGAN WITH CHERRY SOUP
Poems and Stories by Linda J. Albertano and Frank Lutz;
Foreword by Susan Hayden

This companion book to *On the Life of Linda J. Albertano*, offers a retrospective of Linda and Frank's written work, including poetry and prose, providing a fascinating look at the creative force that emerged from this one-of-a-kind relationship.

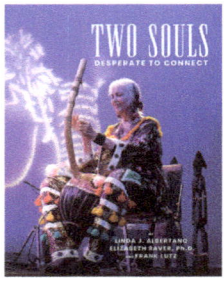

TWO SOULS DESPERATE TO CONNECT:
WITH HELP FROM A THIRD ONE
By Elizabeth Raver, Ph.D., Linda J. Albertano, and Frank Lutz

This one-of-a-kind literary work reveals how two lovers, separated by the death of one, have remained in contact, featuring actual transcriptions of "live" conversations between Linda in the Afterlife, Frank on Earth, and Elizabeth, the Medium who helps them. It offers a guide for readers to contact their own departed loved one directly!

POETRY DIVA:
NEWLY FOUND POEMS AND STORIES
By Linda J. Albertano and Frank Lutz

A collection of never-before-published works by Linda J. Albertano, including poems, stories, songs, works in invented languages and more. Also features new work by her husband Frank Lutz, and color images throughout.

For more details, visit QUIET TIME PUBLISHING online at **www.quiettimepublishing.com** or scan the QR code

www.ingramcontent.com/pod-product-compliance
Lightning Source LLC
Chambersburg PA
CBHW051330110526
44590CB00032B/4472